Rich and Rare

Sir Alan Smith

Rich and Rare

The Story of
DAWSON INTERNATIONAL

by Jackie Moore

HENRY MELLAND
LONDON 1986

First published in Great Britain in 1986
by Henry Melland Limited
23 Ridgmount Street, London WC1E 7AH

for Dawson International p.l.c.
Kinross KY13 7DH Scotland

ISBN 0 907929 13 3

Designed by Ann Ross Paterson

Photographs on the endpapers, frontispiece and page 74 by
Christopher Moore and on pages 13, 19, 44, 67, 76, 77, 80, 82,
83, 85, 86, 87, 100, 101, 102, 103 and 105 by MVAV

Set in 11/13 point Garamond
Paper—Parilux Cream 170gsm
Printed in Scotland by
Blackwood Pillans and Wilson Limited, Edinburgh
Bound ¼ Chieftain Goatskin with Iris cloth sides by
Hunter & Foulis Limited, Edinburgh

Contents

The Author

Jackie Moore began her career in the production department at the book publishers Macmillans, moving on to *The Studio* magazine. An invaluable period at United Trade Press provided the opportunity to learn about fabrics and fibres, the basis of the fashion business. She has been writing about fashion and the textile business ever since, both for consumer publications and the trade press. Writing about textiles inevitably brought her to Scotland on many occasions and her ties with the Scots have been strengthened by her work as a regular contributor, for nearly twenty years, to the *Glasgow Herald* newspaper. Today she writes for among others the *Yorkshire Post, Woman's Journal*, the *Christian Science Monitor, International Textiles* and the *Bond Street* magazine as well as many publications overseas.

Acknowledgements

Writing this book has given the author a glimpse of what it must be like to work as a painter on the Forth Bridge. Even as the ink dries on the printed page no doubt yet another chapter is about to be added to the ever-developing saga that is the story of Dawson International.

The journey of investigation through the many companies that make up this highly professional group proved both exhilerating and reassuring. This is a success story for the British manufacturing industry and the fact that so much of it is based in Scotland comes as a bonus to an adopted Scot.

Among the many who smoothed the path of learning were all the managing directors and the members of their teams who patiently took the author through the mill. Special thanks are due to the encyclopaedic memory of Ernest Tait. Much was gleaned from the *Third Statistical Account of Scotland*, Clifford Gulvin's far-ranging book on the Scottish hosiery and knitwear industry and the exhaustively researched history of the Hawick knitwear industry by Hugh Barty-King.

There must be a special word of thanks to the stalwart band of Dawson women, both those who endured with good humour much peering over shoulders and those who searched their memories to add to the store of knowledge. Led by Lady Smith they included Mary Farries, Margaret Shaw, Maureen Black, Elizabeth Williams, Wilma Adams and, above all, Jean Gibson.

Unquestionably without Sir Alan Smith neither the Dawson company nor the book could have happened. His fund of stories is endless, though not all are suitable for inclusion!

Finally my thanks to Ronald Miller for his quiet humour and trust.

*This book is dedicated to all who
have helped towards Dawson's success*

Rich and rare were the gems she wore . . .
Thomas Moore, 1779–1852, poet

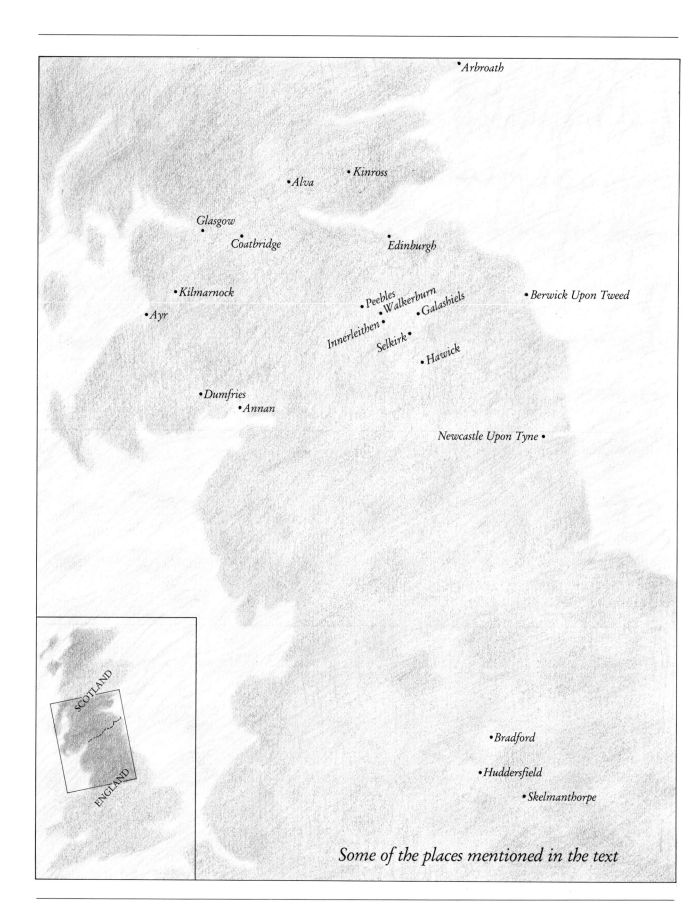

• Arbroath

• Kinross

• Alva

Glasgow
•

Coatbridge

Edinburgh

• Kilmarnock

Peebles
Walkerburn
• Berwick Upon Tweed

• Ayr

Innerleithen
Galashiels

Selkirk

• Hawick

• Dumfries

• Annan

Newcastle Upon Tyne •

SCOTLAND

ENGLAND

• Bradford

• Huddersfield

• Skelmanthorpe

Some of the places mentioned in the text

Introduction

When Alan Smith, the soap salesman, put his foot in the door at Todd & Duncan in 1946 he was working alongside a staff of 42. By the time he was preparing to stand down as chairman, 35 years later, he was steering more than 7,500 members of Dawson International, by then a textile giant.

In between he had built up an empire that included some 30 companies which encompassed the globe and whose pre-tax profits in 1981 were £23 million. That same year Dawson International had moved from sixteenth to fifth place, based on profits on capital employed, in a list published by the British business publication *Management Today.*

Smith had achieved this at a time when much of Britain's textile business was crying into its dye vats about currency fluctuations and implying that every foreign government maintained some kind of dirty tricks department specifically aimed at making the life of the British textile man impossible. Smith preferred to remind everyone that the British mill owners of the 1880s were among the first to get out into the world markets and sell their products. He usually added that it was the American buyers who had made the Scottish knitwear business just after the war. One man's healthy export figures are another's disrupting imports.

Smith led Dawson into trading with the world by impressing on his managing directors the irresistible advantages of quality plus the virtues of investigating and tailoring your product to fit happily into a new market, then promoting as hard as you can. He added the inescapable truth about deliveries, quoting 'goods cannot be sold unless and until they are on the customers' shelves'.

So rare was his brand of common sense that *Wool Record,* the voice of the British wool trade, suggested that Smith's thoughts should be 'put on the desk of every government minister, on the table of every boardroom and on the notice board of every factory in the country'.

When Ronald Miller became chairman in 1982, following Smith's retirement and appointment as first life president and non-executive director, the Dawson board was a tight-knit one, with John Embrey (financial director), Geoffrey Smith (eternally enthusiastic on all things technical), John Waterton (marketing) and David Blackburn (managing director of Joseph Dawson, Bradford).

There were three non-executive directors, Ronald Alexander, a well-known businessman in Scotland, John Bolton, keeping the balance with his unique knowledge and understanding of small companies, and Smith himself.

Ronald Miller not only took over the job as chairman and chief executive from Sir Alan Smith, he maintained the drive and momentum which had always characterised the company. By the time he made his report to the annual general meeting in 1985 he had added to the profitability of the group with a boost to pre-tax profits of 39 per cent, taking the pre-tax profit to £35.1 million. He had advanced the company still further up the business ladder to take Dawson International to fourth position in the list of UK textile companies.

The Dawson group is a flourishing example of what can happen when there are more Indians than Chiefs and when the few Chiefs there are, are picking up the right smoke signals.

Todd & Duncan, Lochleven Mills, Kinross

The Story Begins

History has a way of redirecting lives and it isn't too fussy if it is changing the signposts on the paths of kings or more everyday folk. Every now and again it flings in a war because, whether it be a mediaeval skirmish or the full horror of the 20th century variety, the result can always be guaranteed to bring about the maximum disruption.

It was war that led a young salesman from the North East of England called Alan Smith into the RAF and to Scotland. It was that same catastrophe that cut tragically short the lives of the two most likely heirs to Joseph Dawson Limited, cashmere processors of Bradford. How these two seemingly unconnected twists of fate became enmeshed is the beginning of the story of one of Britain's biggest and most successful textile groups.

Alan Smith was no stranger to Bradford. In 1936, when he was a young man, in years as well as spirit, for he has never lost that evergreen quality, Alan Smith sold soap for Unilever. His territory was Yorkshire and when he visited Bradford he stayed in Leeds Road where he was within 200 yards of a mill—so close he could see it from his lodging house window. The mill had a name carved in the stone wall, the name of Joseph Dawson, and if Smith had not been far too busy getting on with his life to spare the time for peering into crystal balls he might have been given a glimpse of things to come.

The young soap salesman, though optimistic and sure of success, could never have anticipated that he would become the first president of an internationally known company bearing that same Dawson name. Certainly he never gave the mill a thought in those days because he was fully occupied with his soap and very soon his bosses back in Blackfriars, London, thought he was doing so well they would take him away from Yorkshire and turn him loose on really difficult customers, the shopkeepers of South Wales.

He was used to a challenge. Life had been no bed of roses since 1931 when, at the age of 14, he had set out to earn his living, helping his mother run an ironmongery in South Shields after the death of his sea captain father. For the young Tynesider hard work was so much part of his life that he has never seen fit to comment on it since. Indeed, as any of his managing director colleagues today will tell you, Smith has always been first at his own office, whatever the hour, and there are those who will swear that he would sleep in his car outside their office so he could reach it before they did whenever there was a meeting.

Tangmere Spitfire Wing, 1941. From left, Billy Burton, Johnnie Johnson, 'Cocky' Dundas, Douglas Bader and Alan Smith

He was a natural for the Air Force when war came and ideal material to be a Spitfire pilot, flying alongside Douglas Bader and, almost incidentally, picking up a Distinguished Flying Cross and bar along the way. The RAF took him to Kinross where he met and married the attractive driver of the mobile canteen, Margaret Todd, daughter of the managing director of Todd & Duncan, a small local spinning mill. In 1945 when the war was over and the young pilot left the RAF he did not return to his soap but settled in Kinross with his new wife. His long love affair with Scotland and the textile trade began when he joined Todd & Duncan. He fell as naturally into the spinning business as he had into the RAF, although there must have been frustrating moments for the young man in an established business. He spent four months at the Galashiels Textile College and applied himself to learning all he could in the mill. He had acquired enough knowledge when his father-in-law became too ill to be able to cope with taking over the running of the company, and when Herbert Todd died in 1954 Smith was appointed managing director.

Herbert C. Todd

Herbert Charles Todd had died after an illness lasting almost six years. In those days of penal estate duty on family-owned businesses there were financial problems. The very success and profitability of Todd & Duncan in those early post-war years aggravated the situation.

Smith was fortunate to meet, at that time, Philip Downey, a Yorkshire lawyer living in Huddersfield who was also an authority on tax affairs. Thanks to Downey's efforts, matters were resolved and Todd & Duncan were able to continue to grow and expand their business. As Smith has been known to say, life will always have its surprises and problems but usually there is someone to turn to for assistance.

His board was otherwise wholly female and perhaps it was his experience over the years dealing with Mrs McMeekin (Herbert Todd's sister), his wife Margaret Todd and her sister Hilda that prepared him for today, when he conducts a fairly regular correspondence with Margaret Thatcher, of whom he is a keen supporter.

The company he now found himself running had started out in 1867, in Alva, Clackmannanshire, when William Todd, the son of a local textile manufacturer, and James Duncan, a Glasgow leather merchant, formed their company supplying weaving yarn. Their partnership was taken a stage further when William became James's brother-in-law.

William Todd

Loch Leven Castle

The two directors worked alongside their employees the customary 12 hours every day and slowly built up their business until, in 1895, they were able to expand into another mill some miles away at Kinross, built 30 years earlier. It was beautifully situated at the edge of Loch Leven, not far from the island castle where Mary Queen of Scots was detained and forced to abdicate in favour of her son James.

Sadly, the Alva mill was destroyed by a spectacular fire in 1906 and only the ruins can be seen today. From then on, the entire Todd & Duncan enterprise was concentrated in Kinross, where business continued to grow, quietly, selling yarns to weavers in Britain and Europe. In 1939 came the war and the subsequent arrival of the newcomer to the management, in the lively shape of Alan Smith.

Todd & Duncan were one of only seven cashmere spinners in Great Britain. When Smith joined them they were supplying various yarns for tweed and for the military uniforms that then occupied much of the textile trade. Knitting yarns accounted for only a tiny proportion of the total Todd & Duncan production at that time but Smith was convinced that the future lay in knitwear rather than cloth. He set up a research and development department to look into what was needed in terms of raw material and machinery and he led the company towards high quality knitting yarns, starting with lambswool then adding cashmere. In those days Alan Smith's office was one room downstairs at the mill.

Helping him on the production was Charles Stevenson, known universally as Steve. He was an apt colleague for Alan Smith and they saw eye to eye at once. They shared a hard-working start to life, for Steve had worked as a bell-boy in the Golden Lion Hotel in his home town of Stirling as the breadwinner in his family, bringing home more in tips than the others could earn in a week. He was then just 10 years old. Nevertheless, he managed to finish his education, worked in an architect's office for a short time then trained as a sanitary inspector. It was this that brought him, after his RAF service, to Kinross, where he was appointed by the Provost to be the chief sanitary inspector for the town. Smith felt that if the young man was good enough to be employed by the Provost, he was good enough for Todd & Duncan.

'Steve was the first person I ever employed. He was another RAF man so I knew he was all right.' Neither man appeared then, or now for that matter, to find it at all odd for Stevenson to make such a dramatic switch.

Stevenson had joined Todd & Duncan as a management trainee in 1953, studying at the Galashiels Textile College before being appointed mill manager in 1959 and, seven years later, managing director.

Opposite: Mary, Queen of Scots, after Nicholas Hilliard
National Portrait Gallery, London

MARIA
D   G
SCOTIÆ
PIISSIMA REGINA
FRANCIÆ DOTARIA
ANNO
ÆTATISREGNIQ
36
ANGLICÆ CAPTIVIT
10
H
578

A second important appointment in those early days was that of Tommy Ashdown, who started with Todd & Duncan in 1958, straight from university. With a natural flair for machinery and production engineering, he, along with Smith and Stevenson, designed and equipped the massive and attractive spinning mill, turning it into arguably the largest and certainly the most modern in the world. After some years with Todd & Duncan, Ashdown, a fervent Yorkshireman, returned to his native county to become managing director of Joseph Dawson in Bradford. He then moved outside the group and remains a highly respected figure in Yorkshire textiles.

Smith knew that Todd & Duncan were the babies of the trade, so set out to do better than everyone else. He felt that any fool could make a 2-ply wool, or even better, 3-ply, but he also knew that women didn't enjoy wearing heavier yarns. He decided that Todd & Duncan had to produce a perfect single-ply yarn and, as they proved eventually to be the only people to get it right, the moment came when it was practically impossible for knitters to buy single-ply cashmere anywhere else. Smith's prices were higher but because his quality control was so stringent there were fewer rejects. In the end it was better for the knitter to pay the extra money. 'We had a concept of perfection right from the beginning and it was that that kept us going, even though people like Willie Mactaggart of Pringle would have preferred to give us rather less of their business in case they became too dependent upon us,' Smith explains.

Smith's running of the Kinross spinning mill in those days was as enterprising as his later approach to the larger, rather less manageable conglomerate that was to become Dawson International. He was still flying, often by the seat of his pants, and he was thoroughly enjoying the trip.

In 1946 Todd & Duncan used virtually no cashmere. By 1960 they were spinning more than half the UK cashmere yarn production and using about half of the output of the Bradford company Joseph Dawson, who specialised in the dehairing of raw cashmere, a very necessary process before spinning. Dawson had a monopoly on the processing of the luxury fibre. They were the best and they knew it. 'By God they were autocratic' remembers Smith. Yet the chairman of Todd & Duncan had much in common with the men who had made Joseph Dawson and, in particular, with the founder.

For a picture of the Yorkshire woollen mills 100 years ago you need only look at the life of Joseph Dawson, who started work at eight years old as what they called a 'half timer' in an Otley, Yorkshire spinning mill. The average working day started at 6 am and finished at 6 pm and there was usually quite a walk to the mill through the cold early mornings and wet evenings. Joseph grew up into a tough Yorkshireman, quite capable of working his 12-hour day then walking many miles into Bradford to hear an orchestral concert.

He worked hard with the William Ackroyd mill in Otley, making his way up to become a carding overlooker but he was a fiercely independent fellow and knew that eventually he wanted his own mill. The opportunity came after he married when he set up in business with his brother-in-law.

In 1871 he settled for running things on his own, to be joined eventually by sons Benjamin, aged 17, and Allon, aged 15.

In those days conditions in the cold, often damp mills led to tuberculosis and other diseases. Working so hard from an early age had also taken its toll and Joseph became seriously ill. His sons ran the business while their father went out to Australia where doctors suggested the climate would suit him better. He was not expected to come back to Britain but the doctors had not realised just how resilient Joseph was. In no time he felt better and set off home, stopping in India to attend his daughter's wedding.

It was here in India that he first came across cashmere and watched the local women separate by hand the coarse hair from the fine, making it suitable for spinning. In those days the cashmere business was very much in its infancy and most of the Dawson trade was in combing wools and animal hair. Nevertheless, Joseph and his sons could see the possibilities of the attractive cashmere fibre and they experimented with ways to remove the coarse hairs mechanically. Eventually, they achieved it and became the inventors and only purveyors of the cashmere dehairing process that was to make the fibre a commercial proposition, albeit a luxury one. Their processes then, as now, remain a secret.

The young son Benjamin travelled the country selling the cashmere to a sometimes reluctant trade. As he went he kept a notebook, which makes for fascinating reading. In 1898, in one intriguing entry, we read that he visited Todd & Duncan at their Alva factory, to discover that 'this is only an extension to the working at Kinross'. That same year he visited the Leicester knitting trade where he found that, although it had been popular earlier, by the 1860s cashmere was no longer selling. He travelled far and fast, using all the train services that once made the journey between the Scottish villages so easy. He wasted no time. In December he was at tweed makers Johnstons of Elgin where 'it was too dark to see the samples, but must send the range, including Vicuna'. He was in Keith, Friday; Inverness Saturday. He tried a Mr Paton but he was 'off shooting on Saturdays'. Another Saturday he had better luck because Reid & Taylor were there—though 'they do not use cashmere'. Crombie wanted to see the range, someone else questioned why there was not something new to look at, like lion or hyena fur. Was it a serious enquiry, or a variation on the many ways to put off an enthusiastic salesman?

As for Ballantyne of Walkerburn, he called on a Wednesday

which was bad news because it was pay-day and they couldn't see him. Mind you, on another occasion one of the Ballantynes saw him going into a rival mill so, once again, no sale.

His carefully noted expenses are a delight, with a number of references to chocolate. A Kola was 2d, an Alloa biscuit 2d and a hotel bill 5s, but in those days white cashmere was 2s 8d per pound.

The notebook gives other little clues about Benjamin. He was often to be found worrying about trouble with engines and drawing ideas for new ones. There is a preoccupation, too, with languages, with notes on vocabulary in French and German with a reminder that his Spanish lessons at Berlitz started on 2nd January 1899.

The brothers worked hard together and by 1911 they had extended into a six-storey ferro-concrete building, one of the earliest to be seen in the North of England. Benjamin insisted it be big enough to take sufficient machinery to cope with all the production because he was convinced that as the workforce became more sophisticated they would not work overtime.

Pages from Benjamin's notebook

Dawson never did have that problem. It was the new building that gave trouble when in 1914 the weight of water used in the various processes caused the gable end to collapse, fortunately without injury but resulting in considerable damage. Some years later, in 1928, the 180 ft chimney was blown down in a storm but again no one was hurt.

In 1921, Allan Blackburn, a nephew of Benjamin and Allon and grandson of the founder, Joseph, joined the company. He ran it from 1930 without ever being given the title of managing director.

Gradually, the company expanded its activities in wool-combing, then made moves into manmade fibres. Along with the increasing cashmere dehairing business and the wool tops, they became the largest processors of synthetic fibres, a position they

Collapse of the original mill at Joseph Dawson

Joseph Dawson's mill today

maintained in the years between 1933 and 1950 when they moved back into natural fibres.

David Blackburn, Allan's son, joined Joseph Dawson in 1946 when it was a private company, half the size it is now, with a weaving mill and other buildings on the site. Some years later, when they wanted to expand, Dawson took over the street that had separated their various buildings and incorporated it into the site.

In November of the year David Blackburn joined the company, the partnership between the by now Sir Benjamin and his brother Allon was changed to Joseph Dawson Limited. In May 1949 preference shares were issued and Joseph Dawson (Holdings) Limited was formed.

The board consisted of the two Dawson brothers, Benjamin's son Lawrence and Allan Blackburn. The next step came on 7th May 1951, with the ordinary shares quoted publicly and the Dawson family retaining some 70 per cent of the total.

Meanwhile, young David Blackburn had gone off to military service, returning to the company in 1948. In those days, he will admit, the factory was bitty, with four small wool combing sections producing only 40,000 pounds of fibre a week. Old-fashioned machines were in use and the situation had got out of hand, so that output was reduced to the more commercially viable products, with merino and cross-bred wools alongside the cashmere.

Although Dawson was a public company the board, which David Blackburn had joined in 1956, still consisted of the family but by then the Dawson brothers were in their eighties, Lawrence had no wish to become more involved with the company and both Allon Dawson's sons had died in the war.

The Blackburns, who were only small shareholders, could see trouble brewing in the mill that meant so much to both them and Todd & Duncan. Whenever Smith went to Bradford he had a meal with Allan and Maude Blackburn and it was over dinner on just such a visit in 1960 that Maude quite suddenly suggested that Todd & Duncan buy Dawson. Never one to waste time Smith negotiated with the family, who still owned 60 per cent of the shares, and reversed Todd & Duncan into Joseph Dawson (Holdings) Limited, the public company which owned Joseph Dawson Limited, the trading subsidiary, and so acquired the controlling interest.

The Joseph Dawson name was retained but with Smith controlling the two companies and with Allan and David Blackburn on the board in a transaction which took only two months. The new Joseph Dawson company had brought together the country's largest combers, dehairers and spinners and a start was made on what was to become a million pound investment in machinery and rebuilding which continues to the present day.

As well as cashmere, Dawson process many other luxury fibres and animal hair, among them camelhair, angora and, of course, lambswool. The raw material is scoured or washed, carded and combed so that it emerges like a fine gauze, with all the fibres well blended but smooth, before being despatched to the spinners. All this is accomplished by a small group of men keeping their eyes on very large machines, some of which are as long as a terrace of half a dozen houses.

A typical Scottish hill farm

With Joseph Dawson Holdings safely tucked into Todd & Duncan and the future of the Bradford processor assured, Alan Smith had the bit between his teeth. He started to look around, his eye alighted upon one of Joseph Dawson's major customers and within a year the next move was made with the acquisition of Laidlaw & Fairgrieve Limited of Galashiels together with their associate company Brown, Allan of Selkirk. With the addition of these fine spinners of cashmere and lambswool the group became the world's largest cashmere, lambswool and shetland spinners.

This was the good news about the merger. Not so good, in the longer term, was the fact that Laidlaw & Fairgrieve had been partly owned by the industrial group William Baird and as some of the takeover payment had been in shares this gave the Baird group their first share holding in Dawson and a seat on the board, a situation that was to prove troublesome in later years. For the time being this was less important than the reputation of the spinners who had now become part of the Joseph Dawson group.

William Laidlaw and Thomas Fairgrieve had set up in business in 1864 in Galashiels, the Anglo-Saxon town they called 'shelter by the full stream', to make weaving yarns. William was quite an adventurer. He had already tried his luck looking for gold in California and Australia but he always came home to Galashiels. Although he died in 1880 and his share in the business was bought by Fairgrieve his name has remained as a perpetual reminder of the enterprising young man of the past.

The Fairgrieve name had been handed down since the beginning. Thomas was succeeded by his sons Thomas, Andrew and William, to be joined by Thomas' son Alexander, who became an apprentice and attended night school at the Scottish Woollen Technical College.

The old water wheel on the 'full stream' had become too small to cope with the demands of the mill so in 1881 Laidlaw & Fairgrieve had installed the first steam engine seen in Galashiels. Andrew Fairgrieve was among those who formed the Galashiels and District Electric Company and his Ladhope mill was also a pioneer in installing electricity to power the carding machines. Originally the spinners were known for their Saxony wool weaving yarns, but in 1917 the Selkirk mill of Brown, Allan became part of Laidlaw & Fairgrieve. Brown, Allan were hosiery experts who had the foresight to anticipate the good future to be gained from both cashmere and the knitwear market, and a year or two later Alex Fairgrieve, home from war service, took over the running of the old Brown, Allan mill, concentrating on cashmere.

In the early days the Scottish trade used almost nothing but local wool, particularly the Border cheviot. When finer wools were needed they were imported from South Africa and Australia, but because fine wools traditionally came from Saxony in Germany that was always the name used. Laidlaw & Fairgrieve soon became

Above: Thomas Fairgrieve
Below: Alexander Fairgrieve

well-known for their Saxony yarns but then came the recession and what looked like the final disaster, a huge fire in 1928, that destroyed the old part of Ladhope mill. In fact the blaze was a blessing in disguise. When the mill was rebuilt it had electric light, power and an air-conditioning system in the processing departments, the first in Scotland to have such niceties. Alex Fairgrieve ran the company with his uncle William until the end of the Second World War, soon after which his son T Russell Fairgrieve joined the family company; but by this time death duties had taken their toll and it soon was necessary to look for outside help. It was at this point that the William Baird group invested heavily in the company.

Joseph Dawson were the only suppliers of cashmere to Brown, Allan. This, together with the reputation enjoyed by their parent company, meant that when the Dawson group was forming it was natural that the spinners should be the first outside the company to be absorbed. Not long afterwards T Russell Fairgrieve turned to politics, becoming member of parliament for Aberdeen South and later an under secretary of state. He was knighted in 1981.

With Todd & Duncan, Joseph Dawson and Laidlaw & Fairgrieve now all gathered under one umbrella, Smith called together all the other British spinners and pointed out to them that the new group would not be cut-throat but was out to improve quality, which would be better for them all in the long run. The major effect of the union was to stabilise the cost of cashmere, keeping the price unchanged from 1961-1972, after many years of wildly fluctuating prices and uncertain supply.

This had long been a preoccupation with Alan Smith, who had been negotiating with the Chinese since 1961. In the years immediately following the war there had been no Chinese cashmere available, nor was there any from Mongolia. Only the Iran and Afghan output could be bought, the latter not of very good quality and in any case in short supply. Smith had taken steps to have an alternative to cashmere in case of further difficulties in the future. The best was lambswool—the real thing, that is. As Alan Smith puts it: 'Nowadays, there are no sheep, just lambs!'. The Todd & Duncan relationship with South Africa and Australia had always been good, so contacts there were asked to sample super lambswool which was then spun and knitted to see which came closest to cashmere. The answer proved to be Super Geelong lambswool from Victoria, Australia. Smith registered the Super Geelong in the name of his yacht, Spindrift, and the group began to build up the reputation for super lambswool which it has maintained to this day, often buying 90 per cent of the total annual superfine lambswool quality available.

As shetland business increased, and with such big customers as Marks & Spencer, more supplies were needed. Onto the scene came Arnfinn Straume, a Norwegian wool merchant living in Bradford,

Alan Smith on 'Spindrift' in the 1960s

married to a Yorkshire girl and described by Smith as a very shrewd operator. Straume had a prime connection with the Norwegian sheep farmers and their fine cross-bred wools. In 1962 Straume's company became part of the Dawson group and a productive but at times stormy relationship ensued which lasted for some years until Straume decided to leave and set up his own business again.

By then the South African wool quality had improved considerably and business between the country and the group grew to the extent that more formal ties were established with the advent of Dawson South Africa Pty, a wool buying company. Over the years the activities of the group have spread wider, covering much of the world. A major ingredient in international success can also be its biggest source of potential hazard—the constant fluctuations in the currency market. As long ago as 1964 the Dawson management was aware of the problem. If they were going to be exporting all over the world they needed help, and what concerned Smith was where should he go to find people who could understand currency, be accessible and have an understanding of quality. 'Since the whole world doesn't speak Scottish we also needed linguists. Speaking several languages, handling money well and honestly—it had to be the Swiss.' That is Smith's explanation of how Joseph Dawson AG, on the shores of Lake Zug, came into being. It was considered a novel thought at the time but it has proved highly effective because, as Alan Smith says, Dawson know the woollen business as the Swiss know money. This presence in the middle of Europe provides a base for selling and currency management and has brought much increased business to the group.

The town of Zug on Lake Zug

In the mid-1960s there were, and indeed still are, only two dehairers of cashmere in America who also dyed, spun and wove cashmere. Much the bigger processors of the two were Amicale Industries Inc, and in 1965 Dawsons acquired 50 per cent of their shares. The president, a strong-minded man called Gregory Shlomm, was not always in agreement with Alan Smith and there were frequent exchanges, often requiring on the spot altercations in North Carolina. By 1978 the situation was at a perpetual stalemate so Dawson sold Amicale back to Shlomm at a profit. Smith, who always enjoys a battle, says cheerfully that relations are much better today and Amicale are still very good customers.

The first chapters of the Dawson story were centred on making the group more efficient as cashmere/wool fibre producers and spinners as well as on ensuring access to their raw material. Links had been forged with Australia as far back in the story as 1956, when Alan Smith set up a wool buying organisation to handle the extensive business undertaken even at that early stage by Todd & Duncan.

As for Moscow and China, they had been on the travel agenda ever since 1961 when Alan Smith was one of the first Westerners inside Communist China. From then on he, accompanied by Allan Blackburn, Arnfinn Straume or David Blackburn, visited his suppliers regularly and established a strong and perhaps unique relationship with the Chinese. This stood Dawson in good stead both in ensuring regular supplies and in maintaining price stability. In return Smith undertook to buy all the cashmere they could offer him, even when it was more than the group needed. During the late 1960s, at the height of the takeover fever in Britain, this relationship, and in particular the adventurous spirit of Alan Smith would be the spur which took the Dawson group on to the next dramatic chapters in their history. Despite many promises he had made to himself, Alan Smith was about to become part of the Scottish knitwear industry.

Cashmere goats in Inner Mongolia

The History of
Scottish Knitwear

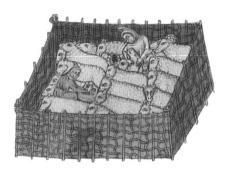

For centuries there have been sheep in plenty on the Border hills, cheviots whose flocks were established by the monks who, in the 12th century, had what might be termed a contract with King David I. They prayed at great length for him and he in turn allowed them considerable pasturage for sheep. They had other privileges, some of which tended to crop up regularly over the years in attempts to encourage the always reluctant Borderer to take a shade more commercial view of life. As well as paying no taxes, a favour not granted to their English brothers, they were not required to serve in the armies of the king nor were they expected to house any of the 'roistering band of knights'. Presumably roisterers were bad news then, as now.

All of this gave the monks time to become experts at tending their sheep, whose wool developed into one of Scotland's earliest exports, selling to the European markets and especially to the cloth makers of Flanders. A cycle developed when wool brought into local markets by shepherds was sold by the burghs who exchanged it for French wines and Flanders cloth. Groups of merchants were allowed to run their own towns, the burghs, from which they bought and sold goods, with Roxburgh and Edinburgh among the earliest examples of these autonomous towns.

Much wool was woven in the homes of the shepherds on handlooms kept in the house, the men doing the weaving while the daughters would be responsible for spinning. As for knitting, no one has been able to say for sure where or when the first pieces of bone started to click. Some say knitting came to Scotland via Spain, whence it had arrived after the Moorish invasion of AD 711/712, but the original Tammy, the felted cap associated with the Scots, was knitted from the 15th century onward and implied a long knowledge of the craft. It could be significant that when the French stocking knitters formed their guild in 1527 their patron saint was St Fiacre, the second son of the 7th century Scottish king Eugenius.

It would be satisfying to think that Scotland did give knitting to the world but it must be admitted that in the Victoria & Albert Museum in London can be found a pair of knitted socks, in red 3-ply wool, which date from around the 4th century AD and they

were found in Egypt. Of course, those Scottish fishermen did get around, they say. Whatever the origins, knitting as an industry was slow to develop in Scotland.

Samuel Johnson, always ready to voice an opinion, said that the definition of the verb 'to knit' was 'to make or unite by texture without a loom', but it was not until someone provided a loom that knitting made any impression on Scots outside the Isles.

William Lee, a Nottinghamshire member of the clergy, perfected in 1589 an invention that had been taking his attention for some time. Lee designed and made the first knitting, or stocking, frame producing the universally worn coarse wool hose. Quite why he felt it imperative to develop such a machine is hard to understand. He must just have been an inveterate inventor. At the time the only market for machine-made stockings would have been fine silk hose for the discerning wearers who would have neither the time nor the inclination to make their own. Queen Elizabeth I herself wore silk stockings, knitted for her by a serving girl, who was described as dextrous in knitting, and the royal lady was known to display her fine hose during more enthusiastic moments in the volta, the dance she loved so much.

Queen Elizabeth I dancing with Robert Dudley, Earl of Leicester
By permission of Viscount De L'Isle VC, KG, from his collection at Penshurst Place, Kent

William Lee presented his knitting frame to his queen, an essential step in gaining the patent, without which he could not reproduce his invention. While she was impressed by his ingenuity she was also concerned that it could produce not only stockings but that other item, one that never ceases to provide rulers with headaches, unemployment. In a letter to Lord Hunsdon, who had acted as Lee's patron for the occasion, she explained why she could not grant the right to a patent. 'My Lord, I have too much love for my poor people who obtain their bread by the employment of knitting to give my money to forward an invention that will tend to their ruin by depriving them of employment and thus make them beggars. Had Mr Lee made a machine that would have made silk stockings I should, I think, have been somewhat justified in granting him a patent for that monopoly which would have affected only a small number of my subjects; but to enjoy the exclusive privilege of making stockings for the whole of my subjects is too important to be granted to any individual.'

Even when William converted his machine to fine yarns he still did not get the patent he desired, so he and his brother James, like so many other British inventors after them, with no sympathetic backer at home, crossed the Channel to Rouen where the French king Henry IV proved only slightly more forthcoming.

Above and right: Mid 18th century silk stockings and a knitted silk glove, late 17th century
The Museum of London

King James VI & I, by an unknown artist
National Portrait Gallery, London

A dozen or so years later some of Lee's apprentices in Nottinghamshire were working away on modified Lee frames and in fact knitting was to go on in pretty much the same way for centuries, until the introduction of power frames. Although the knitting was produced as with hand knitting, flat rather than in the round, a technique was evolved to allow for easy and invisible seaming. Where the fastest of hand knitters could form one hundred loops a minute on her needles, the loom could produce one thousand. By now the machine was aimed at producing high quality, soft, elegant hose, leaving cheaper ones to be knitted by hand.

The first Stuart king James, he who was James the First of England but the Sixth of Scotland, now took a hand. He may have neglected to visit his Northern kingdom once he made the journey to London and the throne but he did his best to improve the lot of his Scottish subjects. The success of the wool trade in England had not escaped his notice, and while still in Scotland he had passed a law forbidding the importation of any wool from England or Ireland, making it obligatory for Scots to wear clothes made in Scotland from natural materials. He did however import talent, in the shape of seven Flemish weavers, bringing with them their knowledge of weaving serge and broadcloth. There was at that time no shortage of wool with all those sheep on the Scottish hills.

In 1609 he took matters a stage further and established a cloth factory at Bonnington, near Edinburgh. Yet try as he may he could not raise similar enthusiasm from the locals even with the offer of a baronetcy. It was not until his son Charles took over in 1633 that there was any action, with the opening of a school at Peebles to teach children how to spin, followed eight years later by the passing of an Act through the Scottish Parliament encouraging the manufacture of fine cloth.

By then it was felt that the native wool was not of sufficiently good quality so some was imported from Spain free of taxes. Still there was little interest shown by the Scottish entrepreneurs and it was only when the Scottish Parliament, disbanded by Cromwell and restored by Charles the Second, got down to work in 1661 on promoting local industries, among them weaving and the making of stockings, that things began to happen.

That same year in London, diarist John Evelyn wrote that he had been to see the 'wonderful engine for weaving silk stockings'. Weaving or knitting, it was all the same to some. It was an Englishman, James Stanfield, a colonel in Cromwell's army, who was to set the Scottish textile industry on its way. He had settled in Edinburgh where he took over New Mills, once a Cistercian monastery. He called upon the help of skilled weavers from Yorkshire and the West of England to train the local workers and achieved such a success that James the Second gave him a knighthood.

He was encouraged to expand into knitting, something else he had seen while in England. The first knitting frames were brought secretly to Edinburgh, broken down and transported by packhorse across the Cheviots, a secretive technique necessary because the rules of the London Framework Knitters' Association forbade the export of frames. Within a few weeks an imported London knitter was at work producing stockings on the secret frames. Right at the beginning it was realised that colours must be 'very current and good, such as true native grass green, pale buff, masareen blew. Noe expense spared.'

Knitting on frames was slow to come to the Border because not for the first time the locals were less keen than their leaders in admiring the example of the English. It was not until 1771 that the chief magistrate of Hawick, John Hardy, brought four frames to the town. Even then it lagged far behind Dumfries, where there were thirty.

It was left to outsiders moving into Hawick to establish what was to become the town's major industry. First came William Daykins, a stocking worker from Nottingham. He was followed by a native of Hexham, just across the border in Northumberland, by name of John Nixon. In 1791, from premises which had been a linen mill in Cross Wynd, an area that was over the years to become so important in the knitwear industry of Hawick, he expanded into wool spinning as well as lambswool hose. About the same time John Nixon arrived in Hawick a young Quaker from the town called William Wilson came home from an apprenticeship to a frameknitter in Glasgow. Soon he had gone back to Glasgow to collect his frame and returned to set up in business. Almost all the knitters at that time were working from home, whether theirs or someone else's. In William's case it was his father's house that became his base, extending into the house next door when he got married. His new wife may have thought she was going to entertain her friends to tea in the parlour but William had decided differently and installed another knitting frame. Meanwhile his mother was winding the wool. William's business went well and in 1797 he built a small carding and spinning mill, the first in Hawick since until then the Hawick knitters had their machine-spun wool brought in by packhorse from Galashiels. In time one of his fellow Quakers, called Watson, joined William and the firm of Wilson and Watson became one of the largest producers of stockings in Scotland.

William Wilson died in 1832 of that scourge of travellers, cholera, while on a visit to London, but by then he had become a firmly established businessman with shares in Scottish banks. His daughter had married an Englishman, William Beck, a master hosier and a most important link in the Hawick story for it was he who taught the art of frame knitting to John Pringle, brother of Robert Pringle. In those early days, though the frame could work faster than any hand knitter, great skill was required from the operator, who needed superb co-ordination of hands and feet as well as considerable staying power. Keeping the thread even as it passed the needles, moving the bar of the frame while at the same time operating the treadles and watching every move of the thread, was exhausting work. In the larger factories with several frames hours were long, even for the children doing odd jobs, and there were days when the workforce could not be relied upon. The hard life brought its share of hard living. The workers needed Monday to recover from Sunday, the day of rest, and Tuesday to get over Monday. As the week progressed so did the feverish activity to catch up on wages. Many of the more proficient knitters decided to start their own businesses, which was not out of the question since machinery was not expensive and in any case you could rent your frame. Whole families became involved, with the children winding the yarn and the wives in control of the buttonholing and other sewing jobs.

Knitters came and went as trade fluctuated. The war with the French slowed everything down for a while and the changes in fashion were giving problems as men moved out of breeches and into trousers, since half hose, or socks, were not as lucrative to make. Fortunately, the coming of the railways meant that business generally boomed and by 1850 Hawick was humming again. To the accompaniment of constant tussles with the trade unions the major knitters had begun to move towards power frames and the Great Exhibition of 1851 gave an impetus to the business of making underwear, including cholera belts, meant to ward off in some mysterious way that dreaded disease.

Knitting in Hawick *c* 1900

The skill of the Scottish knitters in fully fashioning and their adherence to quality yarns gave them an edge in this new market. They produced shirts, pants, vests, body belts, then gloves and dresses, in all manner of yarns. There were silks, merino wools, shetland, mohair, llama. The Robert Pringle company was already beginning to establish a special niche in the sports area with golf and cycling stockings and the interest in hunting, shooting and fishing was proving to be good for business. If the chic ladies of the turn of the century wanted lace trimmed underwear, Pringle could offer them an infinite variety, nor were men ignored since they were provided with jolly striped undergarments.

It was also at the beginning of the new century that knitting came out on view in the shape of jumpers, cardigans and shawls. Though these were originally made on hand operated hand-knitting looms to look like the genuine hand knits, rather than the machine knitting frames used generally in Hawick, this development was to be the salvation of the knitwear trade, especially as the underwear market was moving away from wool and towards cotton knitted on overlocking machines. The arrival of artificial silk, and later nylon, was to put the final full stop to the Hawick stocking business.

There were some who were as reluctant to face the change as they had been to accept the inevitability of the power frame. The first steam frames had been installed in Hawick in 1888 by James Henderson (who joined Alexander Pringle Innes in the company that was to become Braemar). By 1914 there were 400 in Hawick, all William Cotton flat frames, horizontal flat needle machines like today's home knitting machines.

With one of these a frameworker could produce in a day the equivalent of two week's hard work on a hand frame.

What contributed to the future success of the Border knitters was that familiar situation, their refusal to follow their English colleagues and drop the fully fashioning that had made their name. By retaining this and continually watching the quality of their production they maintained the good name of Scottish knitwear which was to pay dividends as the vogue for knitted fashion outerwear grew.

The Cotton frame, with the capacity to knit up to twelve pieces at once, was to be the most generally used machine right up to the Second World War. Nowadays, the computer has taken over from its predecessor, the punch card system, for complicated patterns. Fully fashioning can be organised: even intarsias, the intricate designs based on inset woodwork, can be reproduced by machine.

Yet there is still a place in Scottish knitwear for quality and craftsmanship, a place that has if anything increased in recent years. At the same time, there has been a steady increase in the use of luxury yarns, and the most prestigious of them all, cashmere.

Cashmere
From Tradition to Fashion

Even the sound of the word 'cashmere' is evocative. It conjures up an air of romance and glamour that no other fibre achieves and when it is used by a great designer it can take a simple thing like a sweater into the realms of high fashion.

The world from which the luxury fibre comes could not be more different from the comfortable, pampered life of the designer. The story starts with nomad goatherds, living in some of the least accessible reaches of Asia, high up in the mountains and plateaux of Mongolia, China, Afghanistan and Iran. Their domestic goat is the cashmere, hardy and wiry, well able to withstand the rigours of the intense cold, for it grows a soft underhair in the winter that keeps at bay the most bitter of winds.

Shearing plays no part in the life of the cashmere goat, for when spring comes the soft hair is moulted, clinging to the coarser outer hairs. The goat herds and their wives carefully comb away the soft hair, by hand, gathering the few ounces that come from each goat and searching the scrubland for any additional hair that may have been brushed off as the goats forage for food. These combings are gathered together at collection points to be sent on their way, the first step of their journey taking them across half the world, travelling on the backs of yaks and horses, rafts and sampans to trading stations where the fibre is baled and freighted to the processor.

The cashmere comes in three colours: grey, brown and white, with white the most rare. The Chinese sort their cashmere into the different colours before packing it into the tidy bales that are so easily identifiable with their neat metal binding. Both the Mongolian, in its floppy bales, and the Iranian are sorted when they arrive at the processors. The Afghan fibre goes to Belgium where it must be treated against possible anthrax before going on to the next stages.

Joseph Dawson directors visit China twice every year and delegations from many regions of China regularly visit Bradford to discuss the purchases of new cashmere. The world's largest producers of cashmere and the world's largest processors have established a very close understanding, one highly valued by both

sides, over the last quarter century. This close relationship is of immense value to the world cashmere industry.

Whatever its origins, the cashmere fibre comes to the end of its journey at Joseph Dawson when the huge lorries arrive bearing the hessian wrapped bales which then must be moved into the warehouse as quickly as possible, since the weather in Bradford is not always as clement as it might be. The bales are stacked around the vast warehouses, the heaps of cashmere from each area kept separately from one another and, at times immediately after a delivery, almost reaching the ceiling.

The job of sorting demands at least five years' training, to develop the ability to separate the colours and check the quality of the fibre quickly and accurately.

The next step is the blending, mixing the various quantities required by the customer, using measurements supplied by the laboratory at the mill. The appropriate blend is fed into a machine which removes loose dust and sand.

When the fibre arrives it has natural grease so it must be scoured, or washed, in large baths, at a carefully judged temperature which is warm enough to do the job yet not so hot as to damage the precious cashmere. After it is dried the fibre is taken on a moving belt past the expert gaze of a group of women, often from the well-established Pakistani community in Bradford who find themselves echoing the work of their Kashmiri neighbours so long ago, carefully and skilfully removing every possible trace of vegetable matter and coloured hair, since however small the particle it could ruin the cashmere at the dyeing stage.

Combing at Joseph Dawson, early 1900s

The dehairing process is carried out in machines based on the original ideas of the founder, Joseph Dawson, and his sons. By the end of this stage of the closely guarded process, separating the soft fibre from the coarse guardhair, there may be only half the original quantity left but what there is, is the very best quality.

In addition to the cashmere processing, Joseph Dawson also possess the second largest wool combing plant in the UK and easily the most modern—a new section processing 60 to 70 tonnes per week having been added in 1985.

Vast carding machines which open the tufts of washed wool are followed by machines with ultra-fine teeth like garden rakes which make the fibres lie in the same direction. The final product is called a top or broken top and emerges like a fine gauze with all the fibres parallel with each other and all foreign matter removed. Much of the super lambswool goes to Todd & Duncan and Laidlaw & Fairgrieve in addition to spinners all over the world.

Combing at Joseph Dawson today

At Joseph Dawson, as everywhere in the group, quality control is vital. In the well-equipped laboratory the highly trained staff are constantly checking, counting the hairs in any one sample of spun cashmere, taken at random as the production is going through, to make sure that the hair count is always what it should be. This laboratory is highly regarded internationally and a regular flow of queries comes from all over the world. Dawson customers are everywhere, certainly not confined to the group, with hundreds of tonnes a year going abroad, and wherever there is someone using cashmere the name of Dawson is associated with high quality and expert knowledge.

From its earliest days, when the goat brushes against the scrub to the moment it finishes its processing at Dawson, every scrap of the precious fibre is gathered up, for this is, after all, one of the most expensive products of nature. At Joseph Dawson the fibre picked up from the floor or gathered from the machine is returned to the blending department to start the journey all over again. Cashmere deserves special attention, and it receives it, with the humidity in the mill maintained by releasing fine sprays of water into the air and by transporting the fibre wherever possible by blowing it through giant tubes and chutes to its next destination.

The same care is given to the cashmere fibre once it reaches Todd & Duncan. The first step is for the fibre to be 'dyed in the wool' and here there is an immediate clear separation between the white cashmere, which will be used for the pale, pastel shades, and the rest. Different dyeing vats are used for the pale colours and at spinning stage the yarn is kept to separate sides of the mill to avoid any colour contamination. Careful planning is needed to avoid unnecessary switching from one colour to another on the machines throughout the process of dyeing and spinning, again to ensure that there is no contamination.

As with Dawson there is a well-equipped laboratory where the trained staff work with their computers, analysing the dye sample for each customer then setting a programme that will ensure orders go through exactly as planned.

Each recipe is filed so that the customer can call on the same colour at any time in the future.

The most sceptical of observers cannot but be impressed by the amount of investment in machinery and attention to quality control that is evident in the Dawson group of mills and factories, with Todd & Duncan certainly no exception. The most modern of machinery is used throughout the various processes of dyeing, drying, spinning and winding: providing vast, complex chunks of metal through which the most delicate of yarns find their way. The progress is checked along the journey by the small band of men who, despite the hi-tech surrounding them, are not dwarfed by it since they know their craft and skills are needed. The management team at Todd & Duncan are well aware that their workforce is their strength and they are ready to give them every support they need. As with Joseph Dawson, when the men are working on Saturday you will find management there too, playing their part in the continuing success of the group. Again like Joseph Dawson much of the production goes outside the group, and a special point of pride comes from the knowledge that by far the biggest export customer is also the most sophisticated, Italy.

As it happens the Italians, or at least the Romans, were probably the first in Europe to become acquainted with cashmere.

Cashmere has long been coveted for its soft, light appeal, warmer in relation to its weight than any other fibre. It was woven for centuries into the beautiful shawls and scarves from the Kashmiri city of Shrinagar and merchant traders are known to have taken some to the courts of the Roman Emperors. The cashmere shawls were employing many thousands in Shrinagar by the 15th century but it was not until the 1800s that Empress Eugenie, wife of Napoleon the Third of France and an acknowledged fashion leader, introduced both the shawls and the luxurious yarn to a wider audience.

Empress Eugenie, wife of Napoleon III
Giraudon, Paris

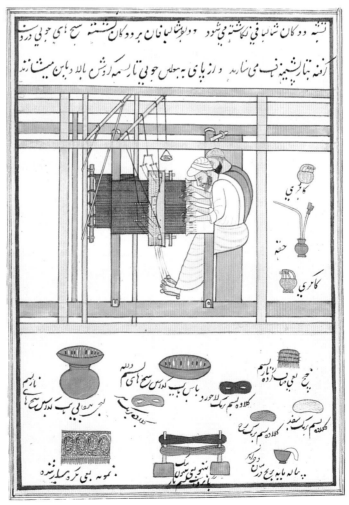

Shawl weavers *c* 1850
The British Library

Chinese cashmere and Joseph Dawson have been synonymous most of this century but there was little, if any, direct contact with China until 1960 when Alan Smith instigated twice yearly visits, following his philosophy of always keeping close to suppliers. These visits laid the foundation for an extremely close and co-operative relationship with the Animal By-Products Corporation of China with whom Dawson were doing business. It is not always realised that until President Nixon visited Peking in November 1972 there were no contacts between China and America and virtually no American citizens in China. Indeed, in the early 1960s even the sight of a European face in Peking or Tientsin was rare and a western visitor was followed by crowds of Chinese, some of whom had probably never seen a European before.

The bi-annual Canton Fair started in 1957 and, while it is still in operation, today most of the major buyers of raw material visit the headquarters at Tientsin and Peking. In the early days hotels were virtually non-existent and with what little accommodation there was, not very good. In 1962, the Yang Chen hotel was opened and visitors found it luxury indeed. In those early years, negotiations invariably took the best part of a week and tried the patience of the Dawson team. Time was not important to the Chinese, although their approach to business in recent years has changed considerably and is much more Westernised. The old Chinese spirit of aggressive business and entrepreneurial flair is well in evidence, with a much more realistic attitude to the problems of industry in the capitalist countries. In the opinion of Alan Smith, business is more easily done today than it was in those distant years.

Today chairman Ronald Miller visits China, along with David Blackburn and Roger Rankin, so the close associations originally built up by Smith are in safe hands and the cashmere connection is maintained.

That astute Yorkshireman, Joseph Dawson of Bradford, could never have anticipated that he would be responsible for providing the means that would, by the middle of the 20th century, make Scottish knitwear world-famous.

Above right: Opening of Canton Fair during Alan Smith's visit, October 1961

Ronald Miller in Peking

The Dawson Group Concept
How it Grew

"Eriskay" by BALLANTYNE of Peebles

THE BALLANTYNE SPORTSWEAR COMPANY LIMITED, INNERLEITHEN, SCOTLAND

The boom in Scottish knitwear in the decade following the Second World War had not gone unnoticed by many retailers, fibre manufacturers and, later, investment companies. By the '60s the takeover fever which obsessed the rest of the business world had reached the knitting companies of Hawick. Over the years these had been traditionally in the care of family groups with restricted shareholdings. Success had brought with it the need for investment and this led companies like Lyle & Scott and Pringle to go public. In this way they could gather in the money they needed for machinery and yarns stocks but it also left them financially vulnerable. This had already led retailer Sir Hugh Fraser (later Lord Fraser) to make an unsuccessful attempt to increase his share in Lyle & Scott, a company in which he had first invested in 1949.

For many a year there had been interplay of shares in the knitting companies and some talk of mergers. Innes, Henderson (later to be called Braemar) exchanged views with Lyle & Scott about such possibilities but all these activities were minor, restricted to the tweed and knitting family businesses. They were nothing compared to the frenzy that ensued when outside interests entered the arena. Once again, Fraser was involved, moving in to buy Braemar and Ballantyne of Innerleithen, but by 1964 he had moved out again, relinquishing them both to the William Baird company for £2 million. In that same year, Wolsey took over Lyle & Scott, fighting off Fraser (with his company Scottish & Universal Investments) as well as Stanley Field (of the William Baird company), while Jaeger took over James Renwick Limited.

The real fight emerged in the following few years, when the big boys joined the fray. Coats, Paton took over Jaeger; Illingworth Morris, the Yorkshire textile group, bought Hawick Hosiery and Courtaulds took Wolsey, plus their subsidiary Lyle & Scott.

The oldest knitters in Hawick, William Wilson & Sons, that Quaker company founded in 1789, could not face up to the combination of recession and competition and, to everyone's dismay, went into liquidation. Their neighbours Pringle of Scotland added the Wilson building to their own and sat, as the top prize, waiting for trouble.

All the contenders, now joined by Debenhams, were talked about as potential buyers but Willie Mactaggart, the joint managing director of Pringle with Otto Weisz, was ready for them. 'If a bid is made' he said 'they will get a dusty answer.' In the meantime, moves were being made towards another top name in knitwear. The details emerged one Friday evening in 1966 when Alan Smith received a telephone call. It was from John Turnbull, the managing director of Barrie Knitwear, one of Todd & Duncan's largest customers, telling him that Yorkshire Fine Spinners were about to take over his company. Yorkshire Fine Spinners are now out of business but at the time they were competitors of Todd & Duncan. Smith was shocked at the news, especially since he had helped keep Barrie afloat at times by financing the yarn stock, but he was not too taken aback to think straight. He told Turnbull in no uncertain terms that he was to do nothing until the following day. Smith was up at the crack of dawn and by 9.30 am on that Saturday he was at the Barrie premises in Hawick. By noon he had bought his first knitting company.

Barrie's story had begun in 1903, when Walter S Barrie and Robert Kersel became partners, manufacturing 'ladies and men's Knitted Hose and Underwear' in Teviot Crescent, Hawick, under the name Barrie and Kersel. Kersel retired in 1920 and Adam Barrie, who succeeded his father as director, died in 1937, leaving John Turnbull as sole partner. During the intervening years the company had extended its activities into fully fashioned outerwear and after the war Turnbull beat a determined path to the overseas market.

By 1962 the company name had become Barrie Knitwear Limited and business was doing so well that the factory in Hawick was expanded and modernised, while another factory was opened in Annan, Dumfriesshire. Barrie went from strength to strength after it became part of Dawson International, so much so that the original Teviot Crescent factory was outgrown. Burnfoot, on the outskirts of Hawick, was chosen as the site for the new unit, and today the factory and offices continue to fill what remains of the space, with the current managing director George Peden eyeing the adjoining area with a speculative glance, noting that there is sufficient space to double the factory and have the machines working 24 hours a day.

Barrie has always produced men of imagination and inspiration beginning with Walter Barrie who was Provost of Hawick from 1893 to 1896. James Redpath, who led the company so successfully after it became a member of Dawson International until he retired in 1978, following 52 years with the company, was awarded the Order of the British Empire in recognition of his services to exports.

The knitwear business does seem to have more than its fair share of splendid characters and one of them, Willie Mactaggart of

Walter S. Barrie

Robert Kersel

Pringle of Scotland board, 1969. From left, Ernest Tait, Stuart Beaty, Willie Mactaggart, Maurice Turnbull, Otto Weisz, Allan Hobkirk and Bruce Mactaggart

Pringle, needed all his strength of character by the end of 1967. So did another of the trade's leaders, Alan Smith. With the takeover by Coats, Paton of the Jaeger knitwear company of James Renwick Limited, Todd & Duncan had lost some £250,000 worth of yarn sales a year. It began to look very much as though their major customer Pringle were about to be swallowed up in the same way.

Alan Smith was well known to the Pringle board since he had been in and out of their premises for years and knew most of the staff. He met with the Pringle directors to discuss what steps they could take that would be best for both their companies. Smith decided to make an offer for the knitters. Although the Pringle board were none too happy about being taken over at all, they did at least know Smith and, even more important, he knew the knitting business. After some agonising they advised their shareholders to accept the offer and go into the Dawson fold.

Mactaggart had always believed in keeping his workforce informed so, through the *Pringle Bulletin,* he explained exactly the situation in which both Pringle and Todd & Duncan found themselves. On the whole, the staff were not worried. Mary Farries was Mactaggart's secretary at the time and her explanation of this lack of concern is that everyone knew Alan Smith as a good friend of Mactaggart. They all felt they knew him personally so it was like being taken over by a member of the family.

Now the Dawson group found themselves not only in the knitwear business but responsible for the future of the Hawick company with the most awe-inspiring past.

At much the same time that William Lee was wrestling with his stocking frame and the seven Flemish weavers were trying to accustom themselves to their new Scottish home, the entry to Hawick from the north was via the road now known as Walter's Wynd. Those who arrived from the south eastern side of the little town came down the Cross Wynd.

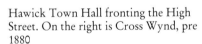

Hawick Town Hall fronting the High Street. On the right is Cross Wynd, pre 1880

It is not insignificant that both Wynds became sites for mills belonging to Robert Pringle, for Pringle and Hawick have become synonymous. There have been Pringles in Hawick certainly since the 1600s, since a bible washed up on the banks of the Tweed during the Hawick Flood of 1767 bears the signature of Pringle alongside the date of 1690. There were the names of other later owners, Thomas and Robert, and at the time Thomas is thought to have been living in the part of the town known as Sandbed, where he survived the flood as it washed over the old Kirkstile Bridge only to die in another display of freak weather, a raging snowstorm. It was his grandson John who was, at the age of 16, indentured as an apprentice to William Beck, to learn the mysteries of the stocking frame. It was probably John who, along with his partners Waldie, Elliot and Oliver, opened an account with the British Linen Company Bank. The war with France was bringing desperate hardship to England, where the stocking makers were on

William Beck's premises in Hawick

J. Pringle's Indenture with William Beck

half pay, but as the Luddites (the followers of a Leicester framework knitter who assumed the name of General Ned Ludd) damaged the frames in England, they were providing the foundations for the knitwear industry over the Border. What had caused the problems in England had been cheap manufacture and, noting this, the Scots stocking men realised that they must maintain their quality if they were to survive.

When peace came in 1815, after the battle of Waterloo, the news reached Hawick a week late. The town may have had its first oil lamp street lighting, but there was then, as can be sensed at times now, the same laid back attitude to news among the Borderers. The Pringle brothers were delighted at the end of the war for by now Robert Pringle had become a fully fledged framework knitter at the age of 20 and had joined his older brother John, a John Waldie (presumably related to the original George Waldie) and a Peter Wilson, with 10 years' experience as a knitter. Elliott had gone, no doubt to be involved with the setting up of William Elliott & Son in 1823, but there is no more trace of Mr Oliver.

The Whisky House Mill in Slitrig Crescent stood next to the distilleries, built under a grant of land by the main Hawick landowner, the Duke of Buccleuch, to a William Richardson for the weaving of blue cloth and 'duffle' cloth for petticoats and carpets. The building is still there today, a reminder that this was the first real home for the Pringles who, with their partners, bought their machinery, including some of Samuel Crompton's mule jennies, with the aid of a grant from the Board of Trustees, set up to encourage the Scottish textile industry. The new company used worsted and lambswool and with the aid of double shifts worked day and night.

By 1826, J & W Waldie & Sons had set up at Whisky House Mill; the name Peter Wilson & Sons was seen up over another establishment and Robert Pringle was operating on his own, becoming one of the first to buy the latest broad frames that could produce wider knitting, opening the way to a more versatile approach to knitted garments.

The opening of the railway link with Edinburgh in 1849 brought supplies of coal for the steam engines coming into the trade and, ironically, a big demand for cholera belts to cope with the disease which accompanied the arrival of the trains.

Walter Pringle joined his father's company which was one of the major manufacturers in the town by 1869 when it moved into a converted brewery on Walter's Wynd, named the Rodono Mill. The real business of knitting came to Hawick with factories, regular hours and an organised system of production. Some hated the idea, preferring to retain their own hand frames at home; and Bill Mitchell, who retired from Pringle in 1952, could remember this practise still going on when he joined Pringle as a boy of 15 in 1900.

Many refinements to the knitting frames and processes were to develop pell-mell over the next few years, all to be taken up and used with success by the Pringle partnership and as the first decade of the 20th century ended Pringle was well into outerwear with their Norfolk jackets and steamer coats. Robert Pringle, who had joined his father Walter in 1885 to be followed by his brother Douglas, added silk to the range and developed the interest in the colours that were becoming so important. Sadly, his own son was to die at Passchendale in 1917 and, as Douglas had no children, the Pringle presence was to disappear though the name remained.

Robert had been the link with the old days. He could remember being carried around the Cross Wynd warehouse by the forewoman Sarah Scott. He reported to work as an apprentice at 6 am every day to be taught how to use the hand frame for the great wage of five shillings a week. The manager of the mill at that time was Walter Scott, who left to form a knitting company with a Mr Lyle. Robert was woken at 5.20 each morning except Sunday and was often so tired that he fell asleep among the yarn and it was no doubt this experience that led him to encourage the company to change the starting time to 8 am, soon to be the standard in the knitting factories.

By the mid 1920s Robert stood aside, in the role as chairman, to allow space for two bright young men to develop as trainee managers. Their names were Willie Mactaggart and Arthur Oddy and it was their ability plus the arrival of a 27-year old designer called Otto Weisz, a Jewish refugee from Austria who had been working with the highly regarded knitting designer Bernhard Altmann in Vienna, that took Pringle to the pinnacles of knitting design. A Hawick man, Mactaggart had joined Pringle as an apprentice in 1925 and in only seven years he was on the board to become joint managing director with Arthur Oddy the following year.

After the war Arthur Oddy left to join the David Ballantyne group of companies and Willie Mactaggart became managing director of Pringle. With Otto Weisz and financial director Ernest Tait, who took care of a diversity of responsibilities ranging from union negotiations to raising finance, to say nothing of showing the promotional films, he led the company, which received the Royal Warrant from Her Majesty Queen Elizabeth the Queen Mother in 1948 and Her Majesty Queen Elizabeth in 1956. The first of several Queen's Awards to Industry was granted in 1966.

The business had been run as a partnership until 1922, when Robert Pringle & Son Limited was formed, followed in 1959 by the change to Pringle of Scotland, becoming a public company the following year. The old Rodono Mill had been badly damaged by fire in 1939 to be rebuilt almost immediately and in 1949 a four-storey extension was begun, to be further extended over the years. In 1954 a big advance was made when a new 12-division Centre Control Frame was installed, the first in Scotland and the biggest single advance in the production of knitwear since Cotton's Patent power frame of the 1880s. In 1962 a former tweed mill, Glebe Mill, was purchased to accommodate the growing menswear business, and, two years later, was formally opened by the Rt Hon Edward Heath MP, then secretary of state for industry. Willie Mactaggart was awarded the CBE in the Queen's Birthday honours list in 1962.

The Dawson group may have saved their relationship with the customer that bought a third of their yarn, amounting to some £1 million, from Todd & Duncan, but it could have been a difficult time for them both when Pringle, the fiercely independent company and one of the oldest in Hawick, was absorbed by their new owners. That the transfer went so smoothly was in great part due to the mutual respect between Alan Smith of Dawson and the Pringle chairman.

As a young man Mactaggart had taken the prestigious role of Cornet in Hawick, leading the traditional ride through the town that commemorates a local victory against the English in times past. It is a great honour to be chosen for this role. The Third Statistical Account of Scotland regarding the Counties of Peebles and Selkirk quotes: 'No better evidence for a young man's popularity and standing in the town exists than his election to the much sought office of Cornet'. Yet, his secretary for many years, Mary Farries, points out that in his business life he was 'not the kind of man who would always be trying to be Cornet'. He had long been a keen supporter of rugby and he knew the value of teamwork, which he said was the major ingredient in the Pringle success. Good relations between management and workforce was

Hawick Common Riding

his constant aim. 'At Pringle' he once explained, 'we never give orders. We just ask for things to be done and expect them to be done with nothing more said.' They always were, because Mactaggart inspired an extraordinary loyalty in his staff. His leadership, together with Otto Weisz and Ernest Tait, meant that the company boomed in the years between 1950 and 1965. Under the Dawson banner, with the pressure of the takeover out of the way, the same team continued to build the Pringle name.

Within a year Barrie and Pringle were joined by McGeorge, the Dumfries company run by Robert McGeorge, the only man who had ever told Alan Smith to 'get lost'.

There had always been a certain coolness between the knitters of Hawick and Dumfries. After all, reasoned the men of Dumfries, they had been far ahead of the Border town, with more frames and a stocking industry, when Hawick was still only thinking about knitting. Nevertheless, when the Hawick frameworkers went on strike in 1819 the Dumfries knitters donated a shilling a week each for their striking colleagues. A Robert McGeorge of Irongray, Dumfriesshire, employed a few stocking makers in the early 1800s and also supplied the local knitters with iron wire needles until these were replaced by steel. His son George made stockings at Maxwelltown, Dumfries between 1854 and 1866 but bad trading conditions forced him to close. Another son, James, had travelled to Ghent to learn more about the knitting business and when he returned home in 1881 he and his brother David took over a small company and introduced the hand-operated Lamb flat knit machines, which women could handle.

The Dumfries companies did not have the problems experienced on the Borders, where men had to be found employment on the frames if they were to be persuaded not to move away to gain work. The men would not accept their wives working if they were not. By keeping the men in jobs, the mills could then also employ the wives, giving them a double workforce. In later years this was to lead to union agreements to restrict manufacture to the Hawick area to preserve jobs in the Borders, with a resulting shortage of labour, something which had to be changed against a background of union unrest in more recent days.

James McGeorge started to make woollen gloves in 1885 and achieved enough success with them by the turn of the century to have more than 100 frames adapted to make fingers. Six years later, by which time he had moved to Nithsdale Mills, there were 800 workers producing gloves, stockings and neckties in cotton or silk, with a further 60 making fancy hose at Sanquhar. By the 1920s McGeorge had become involved with outerwear and intarsia as well as the famous gloves and in the years following the war the next generation of McGeorges, Robert and David, were concentrating on sweaters in natural fibres.

The sole remaining member of the family in the business, still

Glove making today at McGeorge

Commemorative scroll from employees presented to Mr and Mrs James McGeorge to mark their Golden Wedding

there after 50 years in the mill, Jimmy McGeorge, remembers being brought there as a child to see what was happening. He has an obvious affection for the almost archetypal mill owner, Robert, who ruled the place with an iron, if somewhat wayward hand, though he will admit that there were many nerve-wracking moments. Not for Robert an organised system of production. He juggled the orders, promising every customer immediate deliveries. Whichever one caught him first on the telephone each morning, demanding their sweaters, theirs would be the ones to be finished that day, even if it meant changing all the machines, which it frequently did. Production was stopped so many times and orders rearranged that no-one, least of all Robert, knew where they were.

Unfortunately, the business of knitting became highly competitive and Robert's Fawlty Towers approach was hardly efficient. Sadly in one way, since the textile trade can ill afford to lose eccentrics in these more ordered days, his way of doing business was not what was wanted so McGeorge was forced to take himself and his company to Alan Smith and the Dawson group. It must have taken this rather self-important man, used to being in command, quite a time to summon up the will to do this, plus not a little courage. It must be admitted that Smith's eyes still take on a slightly malicious twinkle at the memory of this managing director who had been so autocratic as a customer being put into the position where he had to come to Smith and ask him to buy his company.

Next on the Dawson shopping list, in 1969, was the small but thriving company of Glenmac. It is well nigh impossible to talk about the history of any of the Border knitters in the Dawson group without some mention of Pringle, and Glenmac of Hawick is no exception. It is, in fact, one of the newer knitting companies in the area but one based on the craftsmanship and traditions that have become so associated with the Borders.

The company was started in 1946 by a couple of Hawick lads called Walker and it was George who provided the inevitable link with Pringle, where he had worked in the yarn store and as a frameworker. The knitwear trade was booming and the two decided to plunge in at the deep end with their own company, setting up in business with a secondhand machine and the goodwill of everyone in the area.

It was at this time that Arthur Oddy came on the scene. He knew most of the Hawick people from his days as joint managing director of Pringle before the war, and his energies were now taken up helping small knitting companies through his work with the Ballantyne group based in Peebles. He heard about George Walker's plans and called on his friend Alan Smith of Todd & Duncan, asking him to help the new businessmen get started with a small supply of yarn. The Glenmac trademark was launched, with its secondhand machine, 15 workers and an initial supply of cashmere in the mill at Cross Wynd, Hawick, the very same one where, in 1815, Robert Pringle had established his company. The aim was to specialise in high quality knitwear and the company has gone on doing just that, supplying top quality, prestige garments in prestige fabrics. The company was incorporated in 1956 and four years later took over additional premises. After joining the Dawson group, Glenmac moved into the old William Wilson mill where the finest Chinese cashmere, Super Geelong lambswool and a small quantity of camelhair is used for hand-framed, hand-finished knitwear.

Glenmac was not the only knitter to move into the Dawson family in this period because in 1970 came one of the most expensive purchases, both financially and in terms of the energy that was to be expended as a result. The Scottish Border Cashmere group of companies was acquired from the William Baird group, bringing with it Braemar Knitwear, Ballantyne Sportswear and the Ballantyne Spinning Company.

The purchase was made at just the wrong moment since it coincided with a sharp recession. This was one of the reasons behind the closure, only six months later, of the Ballantyne Spinning Company at Innerleithen, putting 15 per cent of the local workforce out of a job and leading some to question the benefit of being taken over by a group like Dawson. Braemar Knitwear was not in too healthy a condition either, since the once most successful company in the area had gone adrift. The sad situation at Braemar

Kit Kat jersey from Debenhams, 1904,
priced one guinea
BBC Hulton Picture Library

was a reflection of the problems afflicting many much smaller knitting companies. Mainly family owned, they had made their names with their high quality classics but in the harsher conditions of the '60s this was not enough. Fashion was beginning to play a much larger part and so was an understanding of market requirements. The decline of a giant is just that much more pathetic than that of its smaller companions. When the company began in 1868 it was known as Innes and Henderson. James Henderson and Alexander Pringle Innes opened their warehouse in Hawick to sell hosiery and underwear. James had been an apprentice to an outfitter in the hosiery trade in Edinburgh and had worked as a buyer before turning to manufacture. He was very much involved in the local scene in Hawick where he was to become a councillor and magistrate. In the first year of business James and Alexander were joined by James Renwick and between the three they had £1,450 capital, a handful of workers and £185 worth of machinery. The trio stayed together until 1879, when Renwick left for Dumfries, taking out capital by now worth 10 times his original investment. By 1885 the partnership had dissolved altogether and Innes went off to concentrate on the wholesale trade, leaving Henderson to work on the retailers. Henderson moved into his first permanent building, for until then they had worked in temporary wooden sheds, invested in Cotton's Patent steam frames and in a short while opened a London stockroom. Under his son Thomas the business continued to prosper until by just before the First World War the company was the third largest in Hawick, just above A P Innes, the erstwhile partner.

As knitted outerwear grew in importance, so did James Henderson & Company. Then, in a move typical of the incestuous world of the Hawick knitters, the company merged with A P Innes, their next door neighbour and old stablemate, to become by 1920, Innes Henderson & Company, by far the biggest knitters in Hawick. The enterprising spirit of the founders lived on. The company was the first to put travellers out on the road in cars to reach their customers ahead of the competition. In an age where designer labels are on everything from chocolates to sheets it is hard to imagine that there was a time when trademarks of this kind did not exist. A pullover was just something you pulled on over your head until Innes Henderson saw the advantages of naming theirs and investing in advertising. The name Braemar was born and such was its appeal that by the mid-twenties people no longer went out to buy a jumper, they set out to find themselves a Braemar.

This was a great boost to sales but not without its problems. In 1925 Austin Reed complained about the supply of Braemars to their rivals just down the street, R W Forsyth; the early signs of a jealousy that was to emerge as manufacturers developed brand names, detracting, some felt, from the importance of the shops,

until they themselves caught on to the advantages of promoting their own store labels. Fortunately, by the end of the decade the export sales of Braemar sweaters had risen from 20 per cent of turnover to more than double that amount. Even at that early stage there were those who complained that Scottish knitwear was too expensive and for a brief while Innes Henderson toyed with some less expensive cut and sewn styles under the name Kumfy. They were undoubtedly happiest, though, with their top fashion range and they showed considerable skill with their designs. Quick off the mark with the twinset, popularised by the Paris designers Chanel and Patou, Braemar were the first to embroider sweaters with pearls and beads and theirs was the responsibility for the side slashed Cygnet neckline and the eternally fashionable golfer cardigan.

A hand-knitted suit, 1923
BBC Hulton Picture Library

Gabrielle Chanel left, with Lady Abdy, 1929
BBC Hulton Picture Library

Caerlee Mill

In the late '30s, as other companies caught up with them in design but slid ahead on marketing, Innes Henderson lost both their lead and their way. Even an attempt to stem the tide by changing the name to the Braemar Knitting Company in 1952 didn't halt the decline which continued through the '60s, when so many knitters were submerged. When the big Border takeovers began Braemar was bought by the William Baird group and incorporated into Scottish Border Cashmere Limited but sales still kept to their downward path. What was needed was a new, more positive approach.

The knitwear industry, to succeed, needed to take a more active interest in marketing and technology. Six years after Scottish Border Cashmere was formed it was in turn taken over by the Dawson group, and manufacturing of the Braemar ranges was moved into the highly mechanised premises at Pringle.

Their colleagues in the Scottish Border Cashmere group, Ballantyne Sportswear, came into being in 1923 when it was called Caerlee Mills after its premises, the mills that had been the first to be built in the Borders. The business started in a small way, making woollen stockings and golf hose for men, using surplus yarn from their parent company David Ballantyne Brothers in Peebles who had owned Caerlee Mills.

When the Depression of the '20s began to build up there was a desperate need for something new, something different that would grasp the attention of those who could still afford to buy a sweater. The most exciting idea to emerge from the otherwise gloomy situation was intarsia knitting, an intricate way to use pattern based on the inlaid designs used in woodwork. Intarsia is the Italian word for this type of work.

The company developed the intarsia technique, beginning with the simple Argyle diamond patterns, at first for stockings then for the sweaters that are now so associated with them. During the war the Caerlee mill was closed and when it was reopened in 1945 it was renamed the Ballantyne Sportswear Company Limited, under the inspired leadership of Arthur Oddy. Intarsia patterns were developed to the extent that anything became possible, from simple geometrics, which the operator memorises, to the most intricate of

It's a Ballantyne!

BALLANTYNE
of Peebles

THE BALLANTYNE SPORTSWEAR COMPANY LIMITED, INNERLEITHEN, SCOTLAND designs using flowers, birds or whatever the designer desires. This demands great skill and patience, laying the threads over the needles by hand, following instructions from a coloured chart. With this exacting method of manufacture and the emphasis placed on quality the Ballantyne production has always been smaller but higher priced than most.

The label has been associated with top designer names, among them Bonnie Cashin and Chester Weinberg of the United States and the Paris-based Dan Beranger and Karl Lagerfeld. The company also pioneered a total look, adding skirts and heavier coats in 4-ply to the fine cashmere sweaters, a move which led to considerable achievements in the export market, for which Ballantyne received its first Queen's Award for Industry in 1967, a tribute to the way the company had developed under Arthur Oddy and his son Michael.

Working drawing of exotic intarsia design. Each square on the graph represents an individual stitch put in by hand

Shortly before the purchase of the Scottish Border Cashmere companies the group had begun to diversify, moving outside the direct knitting industry to buy Blackwood Brothers in 1970.

Blackwood Brothers were carpet yarn spinners with a factory at the Townhead Mills, Kilmarnock. A family business that had begun in 1847, it supplied wool yarns to the carpet weaving trade. There had been gradual developments over the years, replacing the old form of mule spinning with the new ring spinning methods. Nevertheless, Blackwood Brothers was housed, as Smith tells it, in one of the original black satanic mills. True, a new dye house had been built two years before but the company needed a vast overhaul if it was to succeed. One of Smith's first actions was to draw up plans for a new factory, to be finished eventually in 1972.

Buying Blackwood Brothers not only took the Dawson group into pastures new geographically, it also introduced them to furnishings if only through the spinning of yarns for carpets. This was to prove a step in the right direction.

As was to happen with other large companies in the early '70s there were signs that some things were going awry, in spite of some concrete, positive decisions being made.

The acquisition of the Scottish Border Cashmere companies had given the William Baird group more shares in the Dawson group and Baird director Stanley Field was already on the Dawson board. Smith came back from one of his customary trips to the Far East to find that the market had collapsed, while at the same time massive yarn and garment stocks were accumulating. Added to that, Dawson were about to have to pay for the fibre supplies arriving from China and Mongolia at any moment.

Over the year changes had been made in the running of the company. The first name for the holding company owning Joseph Dawson Limited and Todd & Duncan Limited had been Joseph Dawson (Holdings) Limited. After a number of minor name changes, another title first came into being in 1974. In that year, through a complicated procedure, a new company, Dawson International Limited, registered in Scotland, took over the whole assets and undertaking of the English holding company, something which has never happened before or since in British Public Company history. The group had always been managed from Scotland but because the Registered Office had been in England, even although most of the companies were in Scotland, it was always thought of as an English company. It was more appropriate that the company be Scottish. The group offices next to Todd & Duncan Limited in Kinross were considerably enlarged because Stanley Field's advice to Smith on his return from the Far East had been to hire a group financial director and potential chief executive, with the comment that Dawson was now too big to be a one man band. They interviewed extensively and found their man, whose first act on becoming chief executive a year later was to instigate

PRESENTED
17 OCT 1974
9790

IN THE HIGH COURT OF JUSTICE

CHANCERY DIVISION

GROUP A

MR. REGISTRAR BERKELEY

Wednesday the 17th day of July 1974

IN THE MATTER of DAWSON INTERNATIONAL LIMITED

– and –

IN THE MATTER of JOSEPH DAWSON HOLDINGS LIMITED

– and –

IN THE MATTER of THE COMPANIES ACT, 1948

UPON THE APPLICATION by Originating Summons dated the 19th

day of June 1974 of the above-named Dawson International Limited

(hereinafter called "the Transferee Company") whose registered office

is situate at 28, Charlotte Square, Edinburgh EH2 4EZ

AND UPON HEARING Counsel for the Transferee Company and the

Solicitors for the above-named Joseph Dawson Holdings Limited (hereinafter

called "the Transferor Company") (the Respondent)

AND UPON READING the said Originating Summons the Order dated

the 13th day of May 1974 made In the Matter of Joseph Dawson Holdings Limited

and In the Matter of the above-mentioned Act No: 00368 of 1974 (sanctioning

a Scheme of Arrangement and Reconstruction) the Order dated the 27th day of

June 1974 the Affidavit of Alan Smith filed the 21st day of June 1974 and the

Exhibits in the said Affidavit referred to and the "Times" newspaper of the 5th

day of July 1974 (containing a Notice of the said Application and that the same

was appointed to be heard this day)

centralised management, so that in future every managing director had to refer all decisions to the newly established management system at Kinross. A team of financial and sales staff began to accumulate in the new offices. No one could make a move without consultation, not even David Blackburn, who had been involved with the running of the Joseph Dawson company in Bradford since long before the group was formed. Most of his time, he readily admits, was spent trying to find ways around the rules so that he could speed up essential day-to-day decisions.

Under the new chief executive ventures were made into the clothing trade, both in the United Kingdom and abroad. One buy at least was in a familiar field. The Reinhold group was in the knitting business but took quite a different path from the other knitters, into the area of merchanting. It moved in a world fresh to the group and into fibres which they did not normally use.

Morris Reinhold set up in business in Glasgow in 1921 as a knitwear wholesaler, but since 1948 the company, under the label Emreco, has been in marketing rather than making. Bernard Reinhold, who took over from his father Morris, points out that the word 'marketing' is now bandied about all the time but as far as he is concerned it means 'to identify a market' and that is what Emreco has mastered. At first the small family business sold mainly British-made knitwear as well as a little from Italy, but for many years practically all the range has been made in the Far East. They deal in all sorts of fibres, spreading their net wide to bring to their customer the right sweaters at the right price. Reinhold has always seen their job as presenting their commodity to the market place at a reasonable price, with the necessary fashion content but without being extreme. Just occasionally in his dreams, he will tell you, he sees himself differently but in truth he has no desire to be a leader. In his defence, he will add, Emreco are still here, selling to independent retailers, though the contraction in this area is likely to be a problem. This was probably in Bernard's mind when, in 1973, he made the decision to sell his company to Dawson. Big is not, in Bernard's mind, in any way beautiful so the thought of being in a large group was not what appealed. What mattered to the quirky, quietly amusing Glaswegian (and proud of it) was the man who was chairman of Dawson at the time. He liked, respected and admired Alan Smith. All three feelings were firmly reciprocated and the two men have become good friends. Most important they make each other laugh. Smith has been with Reinhold on Far East buying trips and in some of the more primitive areas the pair have found themselves sleeping in the same room competing, as Smith put it, 'in the snoring stakes'. Smith has never for one moment worried, however curious the conditions, because Reinhold's luggage always includes a bag full of every medicine known to man. 'Bernard' recounts Smith, 'could perform a major operation if necessary, I am quite sure.'

Maurice Reinhold

Dawson's board of directors and friends in Shanghai, 1978

Both Blackwood Brothers and Reinhold were destined to stay within the Dawson group and prosper but other buys were not so advantageous and were to be cast off along the way. As Smith puts it, 'we went off full pelt, boom, boom, boom, putting together a bunch of companies we knew nothing about'. Some control was needed, Smith was the first to admit, and from that point of view the new management made the right move when they introduced proper financial control. Yet still the fortunes of Dawson International spiralled, seemingly hopelessly downwards and for the first time every section, including the spinners, was losing money. With a bank overdraft of £10 million and vast stocks, the Dawson group was poised on a knife edge.

Desperate measures were needed—or courageous ones—and once again Smith's instincts for survival came to the fore. He had been taking something of a back seat. First he offered to resign as chairman, a gesture which was rejected, so he reclaimed his seat as chief executive, cut the headquarters' staff down from 45 to 14 with the previous chief executive among those to go, then gathered together all his managing directors. The company was entering a new era, he told them, they would now be running their own companies and they would be judged on results. If budgets were met there would be a bonus system, with incentives for managing directors and key executives. But there was another side to the coin. 'If things don't quite work out in the first year, you can weep on my shoulder' he told them, 'but if it happens again the second time around, I am afraid we have to part.' This last was, and still is, said with a smile but there have been some swift changes of managing directors over the intervening years. Equally the companies within Dawson International have performed better than many outside the umbrella.

The new autonomy worked. Most of the companies were very personal to their area and had in the past created an identity in their locality. The management of each company needed to return to this approach and once they had regained their right to manage their own set-up they each set to work on their various individual rescue operations.

Smith has his critics, those less adventurous who resent his panache, the more so because it brings success, as well as those who love and admire him but are wary of his impetuous approach. Yet all agree that Dawson International would never have happened without him.

In 1976 Alan Smith was made a Commander of the British Empire and, in the same year, Ronald Miller came on to the board. Things seemed to be getting back to normal and decisions were being made, both on questions of buying and selling. Investigations were made into setting up manufacturing in Hong Kong to expand production of special ranges for the export market, and finally it was agreed that the thorn in the flesh, the American spinning company Amicale, should be sold back to its original owners for $2.2 million.

This proved to be a period of deceptive calm. The biggest storm was just over the horizon and it gathered strength slowly but surely as Alan Smith and his board started to contemplate their next move. Following Ronald Miller's appointment as financial director in 1978, and in the same year the appointment of John Waterton as marketing director, the board had agreed that they should pursue an acquisition policy but what they bought from now on had to be the best. As Todd & Duncan were the supreme woollen spinners, so the Haggas Group in Yorkshire were the best in worsted spinning. With the growing interest in mass production it seemed to Alan Smith that Haggas could prove to be a money and not just a yarn spinner. The marketing director John Waterton, a Yorkshire man himself, had known Brian Haggas from schooldays and knew that he wanted to sell his company, so Smith, Miller and Waterton all agreed that they should talk with Haggas. Stanley Field disagreed so strongly that he went back to his colleagues on the William Baird board to talk it over with them. They agreed with Field and the result was that William Baird decided to make their own bid, not for Haggas but for Dawson International itself. One of the biggest takeover battles had begun.

With the help of their adviser, Philip Shelbourne (now Sir Philip), then with Samuel Montagu, and the combined support of a powerful group of other advisers a strong defence for Dawson International was prepared. Shareholders were informed in no uncertain terms of the situation. Much stress was placed on the Scottishness of the Dawson approach and of its complete involvement with the textile industry, whereas William Baird was shown to be what the documents described as 'an assorted collection of companies concerned with a mixture of operations'. A strong point was the fact that in the five years since Ballantyne Sportwear had been with Dawson International, good management had meant that profits had increased by more than 10 times. The documents sent to shareholders also pointed out that letters from Stanley Field revealed that discussions had taken place a year before among the Baird group regarding a bid for Dawson International.

With all this, plus three steady years of growth behind them, the Dawson board had something positive to say and at the end of the day it transpired that their shareholders were well and truly with them. Dawson won the fight. The City of London had approved of the Haggas deal all along but what really delighted Messrs Smith and Miller was the response of the smaller shareholders. 'Everyone stood by us, all those little ladies who came to us via Pringle, everyone. We were really pleased' remembers Smith.

Stanley Field, on the other hand, was not. He resigned, as the Dawson board had requested he should. William Baird sold their shareholding and the Haggas takeover was completed for £25.6 million (Haggas had cash reserves of £12.5 million) with Brian Haggas appointed to the board of Dawson International. It was clearly in Alan Smith's mind that the dynamic Yorkshireman, with his native county's typically down-to-earth approach, would be his successor and he was, indeed, appointed deputy chairman.

Despite all the boardroom dramas life had to go on and in 1978 Dawson stepped out of their usual role to promote a new yarn. Called Lamaine, it was described as the finest wool, a luxury yarn that was the best alternative to cashmere yet spun. It proved a great success with the knitters in the group.

A new addition to the group at this time was a small company producing high quality blouses. Hans Wertheim and Eric Jones had got together in 1948 with a clear aim in view. They were going to produce the finest blouses in the United Kingdom but they struck one problem straight away. Though the war was over, clothing coupons were still in operation, so however much a woman liked their blouses she could only buy them if she had coupons to spare. Still more tricky was the lack of choice in the colours and quality of fabrics available to the hard pressed ready-to-wear manufacturers. They persevered in their hunt for good looking quality cloths and the answer came from Courtaulds, who had produced what was to become a classic fabric during the '50s, called moss crepe. There was only one more hurdle to overcome: it was available in nothing but pastel shades. Undaunted, Messrs Wertheim and Jones made an advantage out of a shortage and called their blouses Pastella. Together with Mrs Wertheim they set up business in a suburban basement just outside London with two machinists. Eric was appointed sales director and set off to sell the crepe blouses in an area that stretched from Aberdeen to Cornwall. His journeys reaped their reward, selling to customers who were to remain loyal friends.

Success brought the trio a London showroom and the Pastella collection, with its eye for fashion and quality, could soon be found in every top shop in Britain.

While the group had been taking steps into ready-to-wear, back in Hawick Pringle was in the throes of pulling itself together after a few see-sawing years when the downs had threatened to outnumber the ups. Willie Mactaggart and Ernest Tait had both retired and their experience was sorely missed.

Mactaggart had been with Pringle for 46 years, and he was not just admired, he was loved, so his replacement was never going to have an easy ride. As so often happens in life the loss of the two old friends on the board came at the same time as one of those recessions that hit the knitwear business every so often, resulting in a series of heirs to the Mactaggart chair. It was not until Dawson looked within their own ranks that they found the man to pull Pringle up from the torpor into which it was sinking. Bill McEwan

Rodono Mill

was, according to the ever present secretary Mary Farries, bright, enjoyed a challenge: in short he was the right man for the job at the time. He had joined Pringle at the beginning of 1975 to act as managing director of the combined companies of Pringle Scotland and Braemar and the firm rallied, but not in time to save the old Rodono Mill which was considered to be an expensive white elephant. All the knitting machinery was transferred to Glebe Mill, with the administration moved into the former Braemar home Victoria Mills. Several years later, to the regret of many an old Pringle hand, Rodono Mill was demolished. When McEwan resigned in 1983, ready to take on another challenge in a senior position outside the group, Pringle was again in a healthy and successful position.

Ironically, after three years, McEwan had turned the company's fortunes around so dramatically that more production was needed, since his Hawick capabilities were fully extended. News came that Mackinnon of Scotland, in Coatbridge near Glasgow, was floundering despite the assistance of the Scottish Development Agency. The company was under the direction of Kenneth Mackinnon, grandson of the founder, who had launched his business from an old weaving mill in Glasgow.

The company had become contract knitters in natural fibres, among them lambswool, angora and cotton but no cashmere, using fully fashioning as well as the cut and sew method of manufacture. Mrs Margaret Shaw has been with Mackinnon for over 30 years, at first working as Kenneth's secretary and without, she will tell you, any desire to be anything else. Gradually she grew to know the production side so well that she began to be involved in the design side. The styles required some fashion content but in general they were aimed at a middle of the road customer aged between 18 to 80. It was a large market and one in which Marks & Spencer were to become principal customers, taking 50 per cent of the womenswear. Of the rest, half went to the export market, especially Italy. The factory was busy, the product in Margaret Shaw's hands was excellent, and there was no lack of growth. On the contrary, when Margaret Shaw had joined in 1952 there were 60 or so employees and after that she says, 'it grew like Topsy'.

Business may have been good but it was seasonal and production was labour intensive through lack of investment in new machinery, so that competition with other producers was increasingly difficult. In 1975 capacity at the Coatbridge factory was doubled but the lack of sufficient capital continued to hold the knitting company back. The Dawson takeover solved two problems at once, giving Mackinnon the financial and management injection it so badly needed and Bill McEwan at Pringle got his extra production. The same day that saw the signing of the papers completing the Mackinnon acquisition, a set of signatures was needed for documents relating to another takeover, again involving the Scottish Development Agency. They had been assisting the Henry Ballantyne & Son group of mills along the banks of the Tweed but there had been indications that the Agency was anxious to be rid of the responsibility. Henry Ballantyne himself was delighted at the idea of a Dawson takeover and the deal was concluded, bringing the group into the weaving trade for the first time. As the business world had come to expect from Dawson International, the move was a dramatic one because this was not the simple matter of coping with one weaving mill but seven of them, with a history going back twelve generations and involving twists and turns convoluted even by Border standards.

In an area where sheep have never been absent from the landscape it is natural that there should have been weaving, even if only among the shepherd families, but on the Borders there had not been a long history of weaving as an industry. For many

Walkerburn, Scottish Borders
Scottish Tourist Board

centuries the only contact with the outside world was through endless wars and raids between the various Border factions, so it is hardly surprising that the creation of any kind of business assumed minor importance. There were a couple of mills in Galashiels in 1581 and there were sufficient weavers by 1566 for them to form a Weavers Corporation, their version of the mediaeval trade guilds. One of the Galashiels weavers was a William Balantin, born in 1650, producing, no doubt, what Sir Patrick Lindsay, Provost of Edinburgh had in mind when he complained about the coarse grey cloth of Galashiels. As with the knitters in Hawick, the weavers benefited from the Board of Trustees for Manufacturers who first assembled in Edinburgh in 1727 to stimulate industry via the use of £2,000 a year. One of their first acts was to appoint wool sorters in towns like Hawick, Galashiels and Peebles. Even so by 1778 the Board's inspector David Lock described Galashiels weavers as still producing coarse woollen cloths, principally grey.

Perhaps it was this that spurred the Galashiels men on to win many of the prizes given each year by the Board and so show how much they had improved, as well as to encourage the Board to grant money to men like George Mercer and Richard Lees, enabling them to go to England, especially to Yorkshire, the home of the woollen trade, to learn and to bring back the kind of tools they needed to progress. Mercer's son also went to England to uncover the mysteries of the spinning jennies and by the turn of the century they had arrived in Galashiels, together with flying shuttles, carding machines, water power and a Manufacturers' Corporation, 23 men who met once a year to 'settle such things as might come between them'. One of the band might well have been John Roberts who, though he was born in Bathgate, went to Galashiels in 1776 to weave wool. His grandson George built Forest Mill in Selkirk in 1838 and installed steam power, a dyehouse and spinning units until, in 1898, George Roberts was big enough to become a limited company. A son of George Roberts, named John after his grandfather, emigrated to Australasia and started a wool supply company in Dunedin, New Zealand, securing a supply of fine wool for the Selkirk weaving company. Descendants of the original family remained with the company until they joined forces in 1962 with two other Scottish Border family weavers to become the Roberts, Thorburn, Noble Woollen Group. Walter Thorburn and his descendants had been weaving in Peebles since 1821, but Robert Noble came from Selkirk where he began producing cloth in 1880, later moving to Hawick, where he traded in the Weensland Mill later bought by Pringle. Robert Noble had made a name for his cashmere and lambswool cloths, which perfectly complemented the cheviots and thornproof tweeds of his colleagues.

William Brown was another Peebles mill, established in 1852, and the first to export to Japan, entertaining their first visitors from

Display of weaving, early 1900s, at the
Scottish museum of Woollen Textiles,
Walkerburn
Scottish Tourist Board

the Far East in 1922. The story of Wilson & Glenny brings a
fascinating connection with the Hawick knitters, since John Wilson
was the son of the Quaker William Wilson who pioneered the
stocking frame. John had been sent to Rochdale to learn the art of
weaving flannel and he returned to Hawick to begin a weaving mill
at Langlands, where previously there had been only spinning and
knitting. Power looms were introduced and tweeds joined the
flannel as cousin James Glenny entered the business, which went
from strength to strength.

All these five weavers came together, eventually, in 1968 to
become one where once they had been rivals, operating under the

Alexander Gardiner, most remarkable Scottish/American explorer of the Western Himalayas during the early 19th century. His tartan plaid turban, jacket and trousers were said to have been acquired from the stores of the 79th Regiment (Cameron Highlanders)
Scottish National Portrait Gallery

Below: A cartoon showing Sir Walter Scott wearing his check trousers, 1827
The British Museum

group name Henry Ballantyne & Sons, with Scottish Worsteds and Woollens as a trading name.

The Ballantynes of Galashiels had flourished in the weaving trade through the years but by 1820 Henry Ballantyne, 18 years old and the seventh generation in the business, decided to break away and establish his own mill. At first he rented premises in Innerleithen then nine years later moved to Galashiels. When he came to build his own factory in 1847 he chose a beautiful, typically Border piece of land, with a stream called the Walker Burn running through it. Ballantyne did not rest at building a factory, he evolved a village to house his employees and it grew into the town of Walkerburn. The coarse grey tweed of the area changed as fashion took over and Scottish wool fabric became the rage of the young man about town. It had been the sight of the popular author Sir Walter Scott striding through the salons in his black and white Shepherd's Check trousers that had started the craze. There are none so Scottish as those who no longer live there, so it was inevitable that the intriguing new woollen fabric should appeal to the London-based but Scottish born tailor to the gentry, James Locke. In no time the country estates were awash with district checks for the landowners and their retainers and once Queen Victoria adopted the tartan that was the signal for a veritable gold rush towards the Scottish weavers. The Welsh may have had most of the coal to fuel the steam engines but the Scots had the tweed and the Ballantynes were among those who made a great deal of money, even through the period of the drastic American tariff barriers set up in the 1890s which ruined many a weaver in Galashiels, where 75 per cent of the cloth had been sold to America.

The Walkerburn mill had been completely vertical since 1854, taking in raw wool and sending out finished cloth, using the water power under rights the family had prudently acquired from the landowners. Henry had been succeeded by his five sons but even a business as prosperous as this could not support quite as many '& Sons' so the three youngest boys, George, James and Henry started Ballantyne Brothers at Innerleithen.

For 20 years the two remaining brothers David and John worked together in Walkerburn, but in 1883 David Ballantyne, emulating his father, left to build his own mill at March Street, Peebles. For almost a century the three companies, founded by father and sons, were to be competitors but at least some of the family were reunited when David's sons amalgamated with Ballantyne Brothers and took over the Innerleithen mill originally rented by their grandfather. David's eldest son Sir Henry Ballantyne became chairman of the new company called D Ballantyne Brothers to be succeeded by his grandson, another Henry.

D Ballantyne Brothers passed via Sir Hugh Fraser to the

Queen Victoria and John Brown at
Osborne, 1865, by Sir Edwin Landseer
RA
*Reproduced by gracious permission of Her
Majesty the Queen*

Overleaf
Above: Burling and darning sheds at
Leithen Mill, 1910

Below: Finishing department at Waverley
Mill, *c* 1910

William Baird group and it was when Baird refused an offer to buy
Henry Ballantyne & Sons, Walkerburn and thus bring the two
Ballantyne companies back together again that Henry Ballantyne
left to work on his own. That was when he set about forming his
Scottish woollen mills group. He had already bought shares in
Henry Ballantyne & Sons, so working from Walkerburn he set
about building up a group of woollen mills in the area which
finally became so big that William Baird agreed eventually to sell
back to him D Ballantyne Brothers. He had at last succeeded in
bringing the entire family business back together in a group that
also included George Roberts, Wilson & Glenny, Simpson &
Fairburn, Walter Thorburn and Robert Noble. The group was
joined by British Replin, formed in 1947 by a brilliant Hungarian
engineer called Dr Banyai, who bought an old lace mill in Ayr.
After three years of hard and complex work he converted a lace
loom to weave power loom versions of handwoven Gobelin
tapestries, hence the name—ribbed 'rep' weave and 'lin' the second
half of Gobelin. A knitter, W Gladstone, and a group of retail
shops called Highland Home Industries completed the group.

After all this effort the name of Henry Ballantyne & Sons was

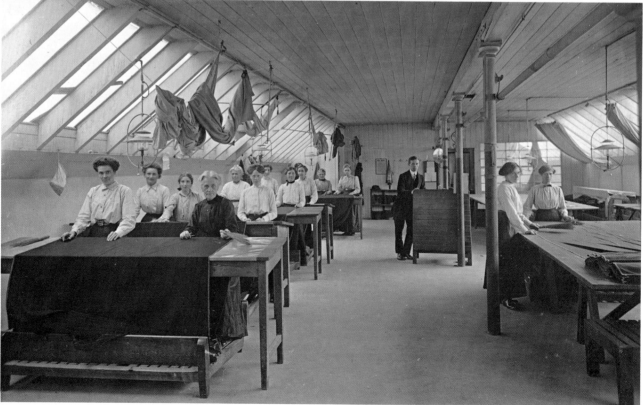

only seen for three years because by this time the wheeling and dealing had taken their toll of both the coffers and health of Henry Ballantyne himself. He and Alan Smith had known one another for many years and once again it was the personal relationship between the two heads of companies that counted when it came to a merger.

Once the complex character of the Ballantyne company was appreciated it was clear that there would have to be some serious reorganisation to make the various ingredients gell. The spinning mill was absorbed into Laidlaw & Fairgrieve, who were happy to have some added capacity, while the Gladstone knitting company at Hawick, founded in the 1920s by John Gladstone, was taken into Barrie Knitwear.

After considerable deliberation it was decided that the woven cloths would be marketed under the Robert Noble high quality label from the March Street mills, using many of the operators who had been employed by the mills taken over with the Ballantyne acquisition.

Although the beginning of the 1980s was far from encouraging, with more fluctuations in trade and currencies than any company would wish to handle, the Dawson group managing directors were generally getting their separate houses in order and Alan Smith and his on-the-whole merry men were to end the first year of the decade more optimistic about the future than at any time during the previous 10 turbulent years. All the extraneous troubles had, it seemed, been removed and they could now concentrate on the more usual challenges of everyday life in the textile business. Not quite, as it transpired, for before long it was clear in the boardroom at Kinross that there was yet one more hurdle to overcome. Though a decisive, lively businessman, there were pointers indicating that Brian Haggas was not the man to take over from Alan Smith as chairman of Dawson International. He would have wanted to make changes, as any new chairman would naturally be expected to do, but one of the more disruptive would be a move back to Yorkshire for the headquarters staff. There were other reasons, including perhaps the fact that he was a man used to running his own show and Dawson had grown past that stage.

No one sympathised more with Haggas than Alan Smith, who could probably see himself as a younger man in his colleague. It was agreed that the Yorkshireman could buy back the spinning and knitting sections of his previous company for £9.42 million. There were those around Smith who were aghast at such an idea.

It was not normal business behaviour. 'They said that there was no way we could get that notion through the financial bigwigs in the City. We said we could—and the City agreed with us', Smith says, with the grin that has charmed many a cynic since those days on the road selling soap.

So Brian Haggas went back to Yorkshire with no bones broken

Raschel knitting at Fur Fabrics

on either side at the separation. One of his companies, supplying pile fabrics to the clothing and upholstery trade, stayed with Dawson. John Haggas had taken over the pile fabric weaving company of Field & Bottrill which had been weaving cloth in Skelmanthorpe, Yorkshire since 1828 and had amalgamated it with another Haggas company, Dyson Hall, rugmakers of Huddersfield, calling both by the new name John Haggas (Fur Fabrics) Limited. The days of rugmaking were surely numbered so in a far-sighted move Brian Haggas had begun a programme of investment in sliver knitting, a method of producing knitted pile fabrics which would offer a more flexible product than the woven variety.

A pilot plant of high pile machinery was installed and the first steps were taken into the sliver knit market which was by 1982 to account for 100,000 metres a week of fabrics for blankets, footwear and toys. The company, renamed Dawson Fur Fabrics and led by Terry Sharp was, with its turnover of £8 million and a compact staff, one of the most profit making in the group.

At the Skelmanthorpe plant raschel knitting was developed alongside the woven fabrics, and the machines were soon humming to produce upholstery velvets, especially in Dralon, in a move that was to recapture much of that market from the overseas producers who had dominated it for many years.

The man who replaced Brian Haggas as deputy chairman was the financial director Ronald Miller, who was known to everyone as the quiet, modest accountant from Edinburgh who had been with Dawson since January 1968. With his introspective, private manner he could not be more different from the outward going, gregarious Alan Smith or Brian Haggas. Yet those who knew him well were confident and, truth to tell, not a little relieved at the thought of having Miller to balance the impetuous and instinctive Smith. Even those who did count themselves as close friends were to be surprised at the deceptive Mr Miller who can be every bit as decisive as Smith when he considers it necessary and whose instincts can suddenly count on matters close to his heart, one of which is the question of design and its importance to the group, perhaps surprising in one with a financial background. That he does not always reveal his innermost thoughts could be due to another interest, psychology, which usually is not mentioned when he refers to his university studies, though he will admit to taking science 'as a discipline'.

His colleagues on the board were not too long in discovering more about Miller's managerial abilities because in September 1982, three months after he had received a knighthood in the Birthday Honours, Sir Alan Smith announced his retirement as chairman and chief executive, remaining on the board as non-executive director and as the first life president of Dawson International.

Sir Alan Smith
The President

When Keith Fox was tempted away from carpet making to take over the Dawson company of Blackwood Brothers it was because he liked the man who offered him the job. He is slightly shamefaced about this rather subjective decision, proffering the opinion that it could be considered a silly reason for accepting a job, but there you are. Having joined the group, looking around the room at one of the annual evenings at Gleneagles, he pondered on the collection of talented businessmen around him and realised that they were all handpicked by that same man, Sir Alan Smith, now president of Dawson International. In most cases Fox's colleagues had made their decision to join Dawson for precisely the same reason as his. They admired the dynamic personality behind Britain's most successful textile group.

Sir Alan Smith is the absolute self-made man who inherited nothing but sound common sense and a passion for selling. He has sold the idea of a textile group dealing only in quality products so successfully that he has taken it to the top. The only product he hasn't really sold is himself. He is recognised by his peers and holds several top offices in trade associations but he is unknown to the general public and used to get much more of a kick when he was mistaken for David Niven. Nevertheless, since 1983 he has been a Companion of the Textile Institute, one of only 50 entitled to that honour throughout the world. He won the Scottish Free Enterprise Award in 1981 and three years later became the Number One Founder Member of the Australian Cashmere Goat Association. He is chairman of the board of Quayle Munro, the Edinburgh merchant bank, a director of the Global Recovery Investment Trust, London and has been chairman of Gleneagles Hotels.

For a Geordie, Smith is much involved with Scottish affairs. He is on the board of the Scottish Tourist Board and the Scottish Development Agency. A Commander of the British Empire, he received his knighthood in the Queen's Birthday Honours List in June 1982. He has always taken a personal interest in local affairs, where he insists that party politics are irrelevant, with sound business sense more useful to the community. He has been a member of the Kinross Burgh council for 14 years, six of them as

Alan Smith at Buckingham Palace, 1982

Provost, is a Tayside regional councillor, finance convener and Deputy Lord Lieutenant of Kinross-shire.

From his marriage to Margaret Todd, who sadly died in 1971, he has three sons and two daughters. In 1977 he married again. Alice Smith's life has revolved around Todd & Duncan and Dawson for 23 years. After 19 years as a lawyer's secretary she joined Todd & Duncan, subsequently becoming secretary to the chairman. An essential to any businessman is an efficient secretary, to look after all the detailed work in support of her boss. This Alice did admirably; then after they married she immediately took over the home entertaining of clients and friends, which has always been an important aspect of Smith's approach to business. Ardgairney House is well remembered by Chinese, Americans, Brazilians and many other nationalities for the warmth of its hospitality. Smith's approach is typical—'for years, all over the world, business friends have welcomed me into their homes. It is always a pleasure to reciprocate.' Outside the home, Smith's interests are his herd of pedigree Friesians on Ardgairney Farm and his model railways.

Now that he has become president of Dawsons he is most anxious that people should not think that he has retired from either business or public life. Where, one wonders, could anyone get that idea?

Not a man to mince words, Sir Alan Smith will tell you frankly he is a Conservative, though as a farmer he is distinctly off the Common Market. He is unashamedly partisan in his politics but does not allow it to get in the way of his business judgement. When reprimanded, gently, by the Iron Lady for a lack of political support in a local issue from one of his managing directors he pointed out, equally gently, that he did not attempt to tell his colleagues what to do on these matters. Characteristically, the managing director concerned did not hear a word about it from or via Sir Alan.

Smith was saddened by the sickness that appeared to grip much of the British textile business from the 1950s, watching as the Scottish weavers became decimated through complacency and neglect. He, at least, learned from the experience, even if others did not. He had been given a lesson in 1946 by David Kemp College, then the chairman of the Scottish Wool Technical College in Galashiels, who prophesied that the Scottish industry would die through accumulating yarn stocks. He was to be reminded of that little problem on more than one occasion.

When Dawson took over the various knitting companies, Smith tried at all times to avoid putting any kind of stranglehold on them. The group lost this relaxed manner of government for a while but it was Smith who brought it back, realising that stifling a company does not help it grow. It has been the same with suppliers, whom he has always treated fairly. Never bankrupt your suppliers is one of his rules and another is never start looking for short cuts because they lead you nowhere. Good relationships have been his constant goal and he is proud of his partnership with the Chinese, appreciating that doing business with them is a matter of mutual trust.

Another saying of David Kemp College that has stayed with Smith is 'never mind the qualifications, give me a man with energy'. Smith says he has never had any of the first, which is as may be, but he is well endowed with the second. He is up at 6 am, swims in the pool attached to his home near Kinross and is off to the office by 7.30 am. Parking his car at the side of the building he sprints up unobtrusive stairs because he feels he should leave the front entrance to his successor. He created the group and accepts everything that has happened to it in the past, including the mistakes. One at least he did not make. He clung to natural fibres when all around him said he was mad not to move into the future with synthetic fabrics. Smith had the last laugh, but then he often does. The group has been successful above all, he says, because the customer always comes first, and every managing director would stand on his head to please them.

Smith has let it be known that he wishes to die on his feet, and have his ashes scattered over the grounds of Todd & Duncan. That might have to wait because Smith has a major scheme under way, an enterprise that is perhaps the greatest dream of this particularly imaginative Piscean. It began when Smith was on one of his regular visits to Australia. He had already set up the wool buying organisation that has played an important role in the Dawson success, maintaining supplies. It occured to him that the wild goats of the Australian outback, descendants of those brought with them by the early colonists, could well be worth some thought. After all, an Australian friend had developed a strain of highly successful mohair goats. It is typical of Smith's sense of fun that he should decide to set up a farm to breed cashmere goats not far away from that well known Australian location Wagga Wagga.

Alan Smith was aided and abetted in this by fellow director Geoffrey Smith. They share an ebullient enthusiasm for a new exciting adventure and this, the first ever pastoral programme to be launched for 100 years in Australia, was just their idea of fun. Geoff Smith has been involved in the overall plan, which was to inject £½ million each year into the programme for five years, check results, then take the next step. The first five years ended in 1985 and Messrs Smith and Smith adjudged themselves well pleased with their venture. They felt they were creating a good industry that would help the local economy as well as, eventually, produce raw material for Dawson.

There are now 6,000 goats and 1,000 fine wool sheep on the 2,500-acre property in New South Wales but Smith is not satisfied with that. He has talked to the farmers, the Governor, and the

Kinross Cashmere Company, NSW, Australia

Top quality white feral buck—Kinross Cashmere Company

Australian farming press, because he is determined to reach the stage where there will be 1,000 tons of cashmere a year for Dawson to use should the Chinese supply dwindle for any reason. The production of sufficient cashmere is speeded up by persuading local farmers to buy carefully bred pedigree goats, with the promise that Dawson will buy the cashmere, or even take the goats back if necessary.

It may take time but Smith has no doubt of the success of the project—he would never have started the scheme in the first place if he had not been sure it would work.

Sir Alan Smith once declared his credo as making sure you control every process in your business or else you are in someone else's hand. Producing his own cashmere was only a matter of time.

The Story Continues

Ronald Miller first came to Dawson International as they were completing the Pringle takeover, a time when Alan Smith was fully aware that they would need more professional advice on forward financial planning. This was Miller's first responsibility and even at that early stage he could see that the group could be developed to grow very profitably. Despite all the traumas of the past, when he took over from Sir Alan Smith it was with the same confidence in the group, particularly if it stayed within specialist areas and a constant watch was kept on quality.

The man who came in to take Ronald Miller's place as financial director was John Embrey, Shrewsbury-born and with the solid reliability of a good rugby full back. Embrey had worked alongside Miller in the accounts department during the early 1970s but left because he felt that the structure of the company at that time did not allow for promotion. He was getting fidgety with the succeeding job just as Ronald Miller advertised for a financial director, so he hotfooted it back to Kinross to work with the man he knew and admired.

The third member of the Kinross management team is John Waterton, a shrewd Yorkshireman with just the right amount of self-deprecating cynicism required but seldom found among marketing men. He prefers the title of commercial and marketing director because that dispels some of the pie in the sky aspects of that elusive jade, marketing. He describes his role as that of trouble shooting, thinking and mind bending.

Together the management team keep an eye on the entire Dawson group of companies, like a camera with a wide angle lens, but ready to focus on a single object at any one time.

Geoff Smith is the group technical director. It is his role to ensure that the best quality standards are maintained both in product terms and in machinery. He is well experienced in textiles and has been employed in the group since 1962, to be appointed to the board in 1978. His verve and enthusiasm are unlimited and there is always a nice meeting of minds between his desire to see the very best and newest equipment in the group companies and the managing directors who, while wishing to have the best, wish

Ronald Miller

to ensure it is proven before they spend the resources gleaned from central group funds.

The team benefits greatly from the advice they receive from their non-executive directors, John Bolton and Ronald Alexander, both of whom have a wide knowledge of business affairs.

John Bolton has been a director of Dawson International since 1971 and his experience in the international market has been invaluable. He is well known for his chairmanship of the Bolton Committee on Small Companies, which reported a few years ago on the importance of small companies to the country's economy. He is also a director of a number of international trading companies.

Ronald Alexander, a director since 1979, has a particular understanding of Scottish industry. His family-owned company has long been involved with transport in Scotland and he is a widely respected figure in the Scottish business world. Many of the companies that had come within the Dawson orbit were family owned, with all the paternal attitudes that this can imply. Some managing directors inherited in the takeover were first class and one does not have to go further than Willie Mactaggart or Arthur Oddy to appreciate that, but sadly they were not typical. Family businesses have an unfortunate habit of debilitating their management and often it proved necessary for the Dawson board to bring in someone from outside. There are still lingering traces of resentment to be found here and there, and a harping back to good old days which were, one suspects, not that good or a change would not have been necessary. Fortunately the group has now

The board in 1986, from left round table, John Waterton, John Bolton, David Blackburn, Alan Smith, Ronald Miller, John Embrey, Ronald Alexander, Geoff Smith and Hugh Somerville (secretary)

been in existence long enough to enable it to promote from within its own ranks. A trainee programme has been in operation for some time to help with just such a task, but there is still no training to beat that of coming up 'through the mill'. Not many months after Ronald Miller assumed the role of chairman he had the perfect opportunity to test progress.

Miller's appointment must have put something of a stop on plans in the minds of his contemporaries within the group. It could have been the reason why Bill McEwan decided to leave Pringle in 1983 to take up an appointment of chief executive outside the group. When asked about McEwan's replacement, Miller said phlegmatically that he was working on it and that he had some bright people within the group he wanted to consider. He came up with Brian Faulkner, who had been production director with Ballantyne, then managing director of McGeorge, and few who knew the capabilities of this young man were surprised when he took the prestigious job at Pringle. Coming after the brisk, abrasive McEwan the softly spoken, sympathetic Ulsterman has commanded respect not only for his undoubted experience and knowledge but for his ability to listen, however busy. Mary Farries speaks of him in the same breath as Mactaggart and there can be no greater accolade than that. The company Faulkner manages today is working in 13 fibres and 400 colours, with a design studio that produces 500 styles twice a year. That takes some managing. His team of designers travel constantly around Europe and meet

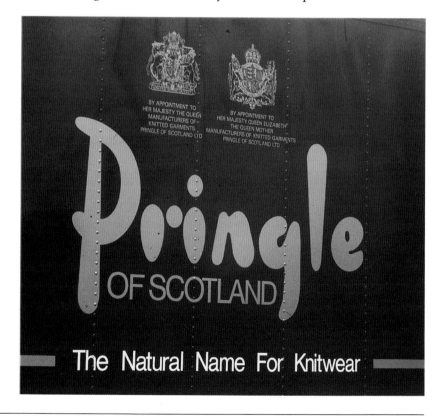

regularly with the Pringle consultants from Germany, the United States and Japan. In recent years there has been considerable growth in leisurewear and the men's division has taken over quite a large proportion of the production.

Faulkner takes in his stride the fact that he is in charge of the company he says is the only one in the world making knitwear of such quality and variety, with five factories and a turnover, by 1984, of £29 million, exporting 50 per cent of his production to 47 countries. His motto for Pringle today is 'Dedicated to Quality' and he is utterly committed to the knitwear tradition of the Scottish Borders. The retail side of Pringle is growing with shops in Dusseldorf, Tokyo and the famous Epcot centre in Florida. There are licensing arrangements in Japan and other countries where the Pringle brand name now appears on skirts, belts, jackets, trousers, shorts, socks and umbrellas.

Though a large part of the cost of a sweater is in the material, considerable skill goes into the manufacture, with some hand work involved somewhere in every garment. Much of the production today comes from Berwick, a modern plant with on-line computers assisting in communication, something Faulkner regards as vital. He insists that decisions must be able to be taken at any time, any day, with as close a relationship between management and workforce as possible.

There are three Pringle collections. There is the cashmere and fine wools collection, then Pringle Sport, an easy care, hard wearing range, machine washable and identified with the lion motif and the Pringle name. Pringle Leisure, medium in price, fits in between the cashmere and Pringle Sport, using lambswool, angora, shetland and cotton.

The frameworkers at Pringle nowadays are all men—the last female frameworker died in 1984—but the finishing is women's work. There are training schemes which can take as long as 40 weeks on the invisible mending side, time which could be halved if it were not for the high standards insisted upon at Pringle, who have come to regard themselves as a training ground for the town. The trainees are usually young people who have the necessary co-ordination of eye and hands.

In November 1985 Brian Faulkner was able to announce that a new factory was to be set up in Arbroath, giving yet more production capacity to Pringle.

The first phase of the project involved an investment of some £1.6 million bringing 150 new jobs. By 1990 there will have been a further investment of £5 million, bringing the total work force up to 550. It is intended that the 4.5-acre site will allow the Arbroath factory to be developed into a vertical operation—from knitting through to completion of the final product.

Alongside this there will be a similar investment of £6 million over the same period at the Hawick factory.

Computerised knitting at Pringle

Pages 78 and 79: Pringle sweaters from Autumn 1986 catalogue

Faulkner has been in and around the Dawson knitters for so long he is practically regarded as a local man despite the unmistakable Ulster accent. On the other side of town, at Barrie, is a truly local boy who has made good. Currently managing director, George Peden joined Barrie at 15 on the clerical staff then became assistant to John Robson, who is now the financial director. George became familiar with management accounts, then turned to the production side, going from factory manager to production manager, deputy and finally managing director. He considered he was fortunate to follow James Redpath, who still drops in to join him for coffee from time to time and lucky to have been for over 25 years with the company, working in all departments.

Princess Ann with George Peden at
Barrie Knitwear, Hawick, June 1985

George Peden is immensely proud of the Barrie workforce,
their machines and their product. Barrie use cashmere, shetland
yarn, camelhair, lambswool and Sea Island cotton, with their
shetland/cotton mix a special success. The machines can produce
16, 12, or 8 pieces at a time, with 99 per cent of production fully
fashioned, in the mill which works on flexitime and at every stage
there is attention given to quality control. Detail is important.
They have reintroduced the old idea of reinforcing the underarms,
and cuffs are made with the seam changed half way, so the cuff
turns back to show no seam. Every piece of a sweater is marked
with a colour dye number, so that even a neck trim is colour
matched and cardigan bands have their ends cut and stitched by
hand. Hand checking takes place at the washing stage, while at the
drying point the sweaters are viewed over a light, then steamed,
measured and checked for shape with even the stitch length
checked. As well as routine checks there is roving quality control.
'That way we get no complaints' says George. Should there be any,
it is possible to follow the complaint through the factory because
every garment has a ticket which is finally signed by the last
checker with her number. The finishing touches are just as
important, with handwritten tickets and pure cashmere swatches
for repairs. 'Our garments are as clean inside as out,' George is
happy to boast.

Despatching is equally efficient, with colour identification files
for each country—red for Sweden—and there are labels for Rome,
Hamburg, Melbourne, Oslo, Florence, the top shops in Japan, as
well as Harrods and Harvey Nichols in the United Kingdom.
Every order is coded, and fed efficiently through the system. 'In to
the warehouse Monday and out the factory door by Friday.'

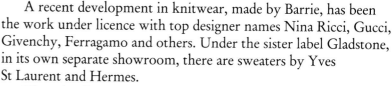

A recent development in knitwear, made by Barrie, has been the work under licence with top designer names Nina Ricci, Gucci, Givenchy, Ferragamo and others. Under the sister label Gladstone, in its own separate showroom, there are sweaters by Yves St Laurent and Hermes.

There is a licensee arrangement with a manufacturer, Maruman of Tokyo, for belts, scarves, gloves and golf goods, all made to a high quality and using the Barrie logo and house check. 'They earn money and spread the name at the same time', George Peden points out cheerfully.

The Barrie team keep on the move, visiting fairs in Florence, Dusseldorf, Paris, with the managing director and the resident designer travelling abroad as well as the sales team. George Peden feels it is important to go out into the market to get information at first hand. Barrie have the most modern factory, the most up to date machinery, but they must cover the fashion colours, design the right shapes, look at the market, if they are to rid themselves of the image that all Scottish knitwear is very, very classic, he feels. 'After all, what is a classic? Today's looks are very different from last year's.'

For each range the resident designer produces a hundred prototypes, for which she is given as much freedom as possible. The new designs are shown, properly accessorised, to the staff, when 50 styles are chosen for the range.

Much care is devoted to promotional material and exhibitions. 'We had a bit of a cheek putting on a fashion show in Florence, the home of Italian knitwear, but it was a huge success' says Peden, who is not afraid to do something different. Barrie decide what they want, but prepare no rules, other than to please their customer. 'I have always wanted to work with the most successful knitwear company in the group. That is what we intend to be at Barrie.'

The current managing director at Glenmac is James Moffat, once a frameworker at Pringle where his arrival as an apprentice at the Weensland Mill was announced, with a photograph of a very young Jim, in the June 1949 edition of the *Pringle Bulletin*. He was back in the *Bulletin* in June 1953, when he was reported as serving with the army in Germany. James Moffat followed his family into the knitwear business and his background, together with the history of the building in which he works, has made him especially aware of the importance of traditional methods. His approach to his work is something that the founder of the company must approve of, watching progress, now that he is able to sit back, in retirement. Over the years Moffat hoarded the old knitting machines that other companies threw out because he knew that the old machines had assets that could be useful in the future. At Glenmac they sell the tradition behind the industry, with garments handknitted for connoisseurs. Though their sweaters have always

been sold in leading London stores like Burberry, Harrods, Simpsons and Scotch House, 70 per cent of sales are to the export market, with France as a major customer. The French especially admire the flexibility of Glenmac, the company they call the 'extra centimetre people', because they can always provide that extra service. The bulk of the business is in classics, with approximately half the collection in menswear, based on traditional lines but with presentation at international exhibitions often innovative. At a menswear fair in Paris the Glenmac display was much admired when an old kitchen dresser was shown with the sweaters spilling out of the drawers, attracting the eye with colour even if the shapes were classic.

For their twice-yearly collections of mens' and womenswear Glenmac make use of all the colour advisory services. They offer their own colours each season as well as calling on Todd & Duncan stock shades. Since only prestige yarns are used the basic costs are high. The equivalent weight of a kilo bag of sugar would equal £120 in white cashmere yarn. Permutating that with 90 colours gives some idea of the investment required. Moffat takes the view that since the cost of material is so high, the sweaters may as well be handmade. His garments have fully-fashioned ribs, and plain coloured classics have pearl buttons. Enormous care is taken with washing time in production, with no detergents but soap to bring up the fine handle. Glenmac customers are often people who appreciate these details together with the fact that the garments are 100 per cent cashmere, made in Scotland.

The Glenmac collection includes dresses and capes as well as the sweater ranges. For some time there has been a close relationship with the Newcastle College of Art fashion course. A recent innovation has been the introduction of a design competition, which offers the students the chance to work with cashmere and get the feel of it, as well as win an excellent prize. The competition is eminently practical since it allows both students and donor to benefit from the exchange ideas. It also helps to maintain excellent contact with customers like Simpsons of Piccadilly, who can use the resulting designs for eye-catching window displays. It is a pragmatic approach that appeals to the men behind this most traditional of companies, which joined the Dawson group in 1969.

When Dawson first acquired Braemar it had looked as though the company was going to disappear within Pringle but today it is re-establishing its position at the top end of the knitwear ranges, particularly with cashmere and with hand knitted intarsias. Such an established brand name and reputation for quality is able to withstand pressure for a while. Despite some low spells in the past, Braemar has its constant supporters and there has been considerable loyalty from the distributors and agents. The name is always to be seen where there is a market for quality knitwear, with the

Alan Smith with the daughter of the Emperor of Japan, Tokyo 1970

professional man and his wife particularly attracted to its classical
style. The export market is important, with cashmere selling well
to Japan and with Italy the number one export buyer. Though
production of the Braemar range has been absorbed within the
Pringle factories there is an entirely separate design and marketing
team. Working under Brian Faulkner, the sales director and his
team are pursuing a more aggressive sales path and, together with a
gradual up-dating on the design side, this will keep Britain's oldest
established knitwear brand name up in its proper place—among the
leaders.

Arthur Oddy was regarded by Sir Alan Smith as the most
far-sighted of men. He recognised that the Border knitters could
not go on producing the same classic twinsets year after year, that
women would tire of them and would need something to revive
their interest. He pioneered the use of pattern and design.

The path that Arthur Oddy set down for Ballantyne has not
been diverted under today's managing director Brian Bain, though
he chooses to hide his interest in such matters as design under a
layer of cautious, assumed indifference. He will wax lyrical about
the intarsia work, which, it must be said, is stunning at Ballantyne
and which can be so complex to produce. Some 35,000 intarsia
sweaters are produced each year at Innerleithen and Bonnyrigg, a

triumph of skill and a tribute to his workforce. He will also tell
you that a Ballantyne sweater improves as you wear it because, as it
is milled less than at other knitters during the finishing stages, the
surface literally gets better as it ages.

In fact, design is as strong at Ballantyne as it has ever been,
with designer Ben Frankel and the Japanese Shirin Zagemi working
as consultants alongside an in-house studio, plus design
competitions organised in conjunction with the fashion colleges.
Knitwear fashion, especially outerwear, has gone a long way since
Lord Cardigan first asked for knitted outergarments to protect his
army against the bitter conditions they experienced during the
Crimean War. Ballantyne's activities have taken them still further,
outside knitwear altogether for menswear made in Italy and Hong
Kong, with the jackets, trousers, silk ties and shirts taking them
towards a total look for men.

There is plenty of activity about in the design studios of
McGeorge. The Dumfries knitters that supplied the crisp white
cotton gloves for the Queen's Birthday Parade now have a designer
in the managing director's seat. Jim Pow was trained at the
Galashiels Textile College then went, inevitably, to Pringle before
travelling across to Dumfries to work on design, marketing and
sales. When Brian Faulkner went to take over at Pringle, Jim Pow
stepped up into his place.

Jim Pow's natural bias towards innovation makes McGeorge an
exciting place to be, and a colourful one when the 30 zinging
shades in the cotton range are flung around the showroom. Small
wonder that in a matter of two years after launching the 100 per
cent cotton collection McGeorge have sprung into first place in
Scottish cotton fashion knitwear. Next in line is cotton/linen and
there will be no shortage of ideas after that. The range already

includes shetland mixtures, silk, angora, alpaca: in fact any natural yarn or fibre that will make a fashion sweater is in the McGeorge range. As their machines are smaller they have more flexibility and can allow for shorter runs than their fellow knitters.

Pow places great emphasis on the image and promotion of the company and is prepared to indulge in the occasional fantasy to show off the high standard of skills that can be attained in his factory. The most eye-catching example is a cable and intarsia reversible cardigan, available to order for anyone with around £2,000 to spare.

At the end of January 1986, Jim Pow announced that plans had been made to relocate the McGeorge factory to a new site in Dumfries. The new factory would also allow for an increase in production capacity by up to 30 per cent. The cost of the expansion was to be £5.2 million and it would employ an additional 140 persons over the next five years as well as using the very latest in knitting technology.

Flexibility is the key word at another Dawson company, Reinhold, where Bernard Reinhold is ready for anything fate or fashion cares to fling his way. 'Never preclude anything' is his motto and with no machinery to worry about he can move in any direction he wishes, chasing the action. A great deal of his success in marketing relies on his keeping ahead of his customers' needs and this means that his designers have to be aware of trends before they go out to their suppliers to get their ranges made. For many years Bernard has been ably assisted by Henry Rose who has significant involvement with those suppliers. In recent years Bernard has sensed that the British manufacturers have become more interesting to him both in price and design flexibility and he may well return to having some of his collection made in Britain. This would please him but, as he is supplying the independent retailer who is in turn competing with the largest retailing groups in the world, he must find for them something a little special. He has been working with the design colleges for some time, giving them special projects and building up a two-way exchange. With collections including anything up to 100 styles, covering everything from an evening dress to a jogging suit, a photographic record is vital and so is communication with his agents throughout the United Kingdom and suppliers from all over the world. The computer, he has concluded, can analyse the styles, the colours, sizes and sales, rather faster than he can and the telex has become another essential tool through which orders can be placed and accepted. The Emreco name may not be known to the consumer, but to Bernard Reinhold that is less important than the recognition of his market. Still more important, he has no doubt, is the fact that he has always been an optimist.

David Jebb needed some of Bernard Reinhold's ability to find a bright side to look on when he first arrived at Mackinnon

Bernard Reinhold and John Waterton

Marks & Spencer sweater by Mackinnon

Knitwear. He had a first class workforce and a good customer in Marks & Spencer but much that needed to be done in the way of improving controls and increasing efficiency. Mackinnon underwent what might be called a period of adjustment. In March 1985 they bought the Coblecrook Dyeing company in Alva (birthplace of Todd & Duncan), specialists in finishing and piece dyeing. With this and the introduction of a cotton collection Mackinnon would at last be rid of their biggest headache, the seasonal dead period, and today the spring collections have become a useful addition to production and profits.

Exterior of Clan Royal shop, Penrith

As well as manufacturing for Marks & Spencer, Mackinnon work with many top names in the British and export markets. In recent years they have also formed a close association with the Clan Royal shops within the group.

Visit a tweed mill anywhere in Scotland and you will surely find a shop at the gate, where you can buy a length of tweed fresh off the looms.

Clan Royal, at present the only company concentrating on retailing in the Dawson group, evolved from just such mill shops originally connected with the Henry Ballantyne mills. Gradually more shops were acquired and today there are 26 Clan Royal branches, covering Scotland from Ullapool, in the North, to the Borders, with excursions into England at Chester, York, Penrith and Harrogate. In some of these the name above the door is that of the Highland Home Industries, and here again Clan Royal is unique. Where the majority of the knitters and weavers in the Dawson family are strictly Lowlanders and Borderers, the Clan Royal shops, through Highland Home Industries, have maintained contact with the crofters of the Highlands and Islands.

Since 1889 the existence of Highland Home Industries has provided a source of extra income for hand knitters and weavers in

Interior of Clan Royal shop, Waverley
Market, Edinburgh

the sparsely populated areas of the North West and Hebrides.

Originally the sweaters and socks, the narrow lengths of
hand-woven tweed, were gathered up by the stalwart ladies of the
Highland Home Industries. There is a glimpse of the life, cycling
around the often unmade-up roads, to be found in the book called
The Isles are my Delight, written by Winifred A Shand, who spent
30 years as organiser for the Outer Hebrides. She talks of her first
journey to the Outer Isles, in 1949, in a Pioneer, 'with a grey rug
bound with maroon to wrap around our knees, barley sugar for
tummy nerves and cotton wool for our ears'.

Today the work goes on but in a rather more mechanised
fashion. The shops themselves have taken on a contemporary look,
with the emphasis on good display and less home-spun though still
traditional products. The rejuvenated Highland Home Industries
approach made its first appearance in the exciting Waverley Centre,
the shopping mall which opened in summer 1985 next to the
station in Edinburgh's famous Princes Street. The Queen Mother,
herself a Scot, had many years ago been a supporter of the
Highland Home Industries in the days when it was a non-profit
making enterprise and her daughter, Queen Elizabeth, was among
the first to visit the Waverley shop.

The changing attitude towards display is all part of a gradual, carefully planned move by Clan Royal in all their shops, aimed at taking the retail group into the High Street. The mill shop concept was of a quite different nature. Far-flung, the shops were in picturesque places but trade was, inevitably, of a seasonal nature, relying on tourists. Today the Clan Royal appeal is as much to local shoppers as to visitors.

The ability to expand now is only possible after a period spent examining each shop and evaluating its potential. Products, too, have been scrutinised, and if necessary discarded. The major aim is to provide good middle of the road knitwear and separates for all the family, of high quality but at reasonable prices, although value for money is the yardstick rather than price alone. Much of the range comes from companies within the group, with tweeds from Robert Noble and sweaters in yarn from Laidlaw & Fairgrieve and made up by Mackinnon. Nevertheless, in common with all Dawson companies, Clan Royal are not hide-bound. They do not buy exclusively from the group, nor are they expected to do so.

The Clan Royal knitwear is traditional in its Scottish quality, but far from run of the mill in the use of yarns, which include blends of lambswool angora nylon, indeed anything that will add to its appeal. There are co-ordinating skirts in plain shetlands, tweeds and donegals, introduced originally with a certain caution, testing the reaction. Their success encouraged the appearance of matching jackets and the range must continue to develop and change like this if it is to retain the interest of the local, regular customer.

The Clan Royal team has been experimenting, finding out the market. There have been the occasional mistakes but Clan Royal have learned from them. Above all, they know they must be flexible, buy cloth that is fashionable and not just classic—keeping in mind the woman who wants to look smart without being in any way freakish.

The same standards of quality apply to the gift items which are much admired by the tourists. Whatever the price there is nothing that could be regarded as junk, no Tartan tat. What is available is the best mix of Scottish craft and design, often blended into a comprehensive range by the small Clan Royal team, led by managing director Graham Russell. Their headquarters are at Walkerburn, alongside the River Tweed in the heart of the Borders. After visitors have made their purchases in the Walkerburn Clan Royal shop there is also the Scottish Museum of Woollen Textiles to explore next door. The old looms and pattern books, together with a reconstruction of a traditional weaver's cottage, give an idea of the history behind the Clan Royal shops, a history that is moving happily forward with the combination of well-researched merchandising and flair.

Clan Royal, Mackinnon and Laidlaw & Fairgrieve are regular collaborators, in particular the knitters and the spinners who have

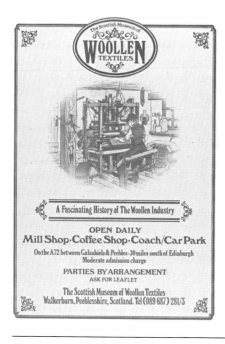

co-operated to put forward ideas for customers like Marks & Spencer.

Laidlaw & Fairgrieve were the first to sell shetland wool to Marks & Spencer and when the new factory for lambswool was built at Dalkeith it was opened, in 1965, by Marcus Sieff, chairman of the retail giants. A new dyehouse had been built at Selkirk two years earlier; just part of the several million pounds invested in the spinners since they joined the Dawson group and in 1980 the company bought and reorganised the Leithen Spinning Mill company at nearby Walkerburn.

Now the raw wool is dyed in Selkirk, then converted in the spinning mills before being sold to members of the Dawson group and other companies in the United Kingdom and abroad.

The key to the success of Laidlaw & Fairgrieve, says managing director Colin Plumbe, lies in the high quality of the product and the service. Designers all over the world have come to rely on the expertise of the team who are responsible for award-winning sales. Today they dream up colours that could never have been imagined and the choice of yarn is so much wider with the lustred silks, cotton and linen bringing with them possibilities for the spring ranges that have transformed the knitting and weaving trades.

Those sales are not all to large scale designers. There are weavers in Italy who buy only a few tonnes of yarn a year. They buy it in small consignments and pay for it in their own currency, in line with Dawson policy.

With so many factories and mills now operating under the Laidlaw & Fairgrieve banner, communication between the staff has become complicated. Laidlaw & Fairgrieve has introduced its own magazine, *Spin Off*, which spreads the news, whether it be of the local bowls matches between the various Dawson companies or the announcement that one of the staff, Jean Smith from Dalkeith, had won the Working for Export competition organised by the British Board of Trade and was off to the United States as part of the prize. Reading through *Spin Off* you see the names reflecting the family involvement in the companies that have existed since the beginning. It is not a trait restricted to the Borders. There are often as many as three generations working at Todd & Duncan at any one time. When the *Yarn Spinner*, their works magazine, wanted to take a photograph of all the various families at one stage, they found it couldn't be done. There were just too many to fit into one picture.

Walking through the old mill, across the courtyard, now roofed over, passing the department Steve calls the Magic Box, where computers break down the customers colours to a recipe or check that the yarn is all right, you enter a very busy atmosphere. Today there are 500 staff on twilight shifts, with ex-members of the staff coming back for overtime four nights a week. Since his arrival in 1953 Steve always had a great deal of fun, but when things got

'Steve'

tricky he would walk out and look over Loch Leven or turn to admire the gardens created over the years by Bob Aitken.

'Steve' Stevenson retired in March 1986. It was fitting that in the New Year's Honours' List, January 1986, he was awarded the Order of the British Empire for services to industry.

This award delighted his many friends both within and without the textile industry and it was a recognition of 33 years involvement with Todd & Duncan, the latter 20 as managing director.

In recent years the most interesting developments in the group have come from outside the knitting and spinning companies, although one, Dil Engineering, is linked with Joseph Dawson in Bradford.

You are never far from an unexpected delight in the shape of a company or a character in the Dawson group story and in the unlikely setting of Dil Engineering you find both. The office of the company is, in fact, in the same building that houses Joseph Dawson and it grew out of the engineering work which is always needed in the textile trade, be it on looms or carding machines.

In the old days there was much to do on the steam engines that stood at the heart of the Joseph Dawson premises. There was a 1,000 horsepower engine, then a 1,500 horsepower version, burning coal and using endless belts and shafts. Dil Engineering managing director, Bernard Gisbourne, will describe the two-inch manilla ropes on the big drums with the same enthusiasm shining in his eyes which peer over his glasses as he had when, as a young lad, he joined Joseph Dawson. His father had already been there for some years, often working the nightshift as an overlocker. Young Bernard came into Dawson as an apprentice engineer. In those days people could remember walking three-quarters of an hour to work, then working from 7 am until after 8 in the evening with only a few short breaks. His own wages when he started were 9s 4d a week. The engine room, he remembers, was always spotless and the men took great pride in that.

At 11 am on the 24th October 1958 the engine stopped for the last time, the whole factory was electrified and that appeared to be the end of that. Nevertheless, there proved to be plenty of work to be done on the machines used in the various processes at the Dawson works and Bernard Gisbourne's inventive mind was soon much appreciated.

He is very much aware of the family origins of the company. He worked with Allan Blackburn, David Blackburn's father. What he feels is important is that there has been retained within the group today a certain feeling of belonging to a family that is an essential part of the commitment within the firm.

That understanding of the relationship between work staff and company led to Bernard Gisbourne's involvement with general welfare at Joseph Dawson and the liaison between management and workforce. His relationships with both sides helped smooth the path for the changes that were needed over the years. He became assistant engineer at Joseph Dawson in 1960, then chief engineer. His designs and adaptations to the machinery played a great part in the success of the company, so much so that he was invited to found and become managing director of Dil Engineering on its formation in April 1974. With his team of 10 engineers he looks after all the machinery at the Bradford plant. Just as important, he is able to tackle other projects outside the group.

The team has a good rapport with the Coal Board and have worked on several assignments with them as well as with consultants and boiler makers. Some machinery can be rough and tough to service, like a coal-fired boiler, but they also work on equipment for hospital boards like Inverclyde Hospital. Their craftsmanship extends to Durham University and even as far afield as Battersea Power Station in London.

With his eager, delightfully eccentric manner, Bernard Gisbourne has the appearance of the typical boffin, so it is not surprising that of all the projects into which he has led his team his favourite in recent years has been the work he has been doing on a peat-crushing machine, to utilise the vast amount of peat in Britain and allow it to be handled like coal. 'Do you realise we have far more peat than reserves of North Sea Gas?' was his parting shot on a recent visit.

If the Pennines are suddenly turned into one big energy field, it will be due to the work of Dil Engineering.

At Dawson Fur Fabrics, Terry Sharp has been supervising building and refurbishing to an extent that would have lesser men reeling. Two years out of every three have seen building taking place in one of Terry's factories ever since they were taken into the Dawson group, with many thousands spent on new machinery. It has all been worthwhile. At the raschel knitting plant at Skelmanthorpe they have recaptured the British market for Dralon upholstery fabrics against hefty competition from Spain, Germany and Belgium.

This has been achieved without any dropping of quality standards or any cutting of corners. On the contrary, as Terry Sharp sees it, you don't have to be the cheapest to be competitive but you do have to be the best in service and quality. Since no one in the upholstery trade wants to hold stock, Terry Sharp and his staff see to it that customers can ring their order through to the factory one week and take delivery the next. A stock colour, which will be going through the factory floor all the time, can be delivered in a couple of days. Annual production is expected to be up to 3½ million metres by 1986 when Dawson Fur Fabrics will be the largest producers of upholstery cloth in the United Kingdom. With £500,000 invested in 1984 in one factory on sliver knitting there are no plans to extend this any further, especially since they are already leaders in the field, although the thermal qualities of sliver knitting interest Sharp.

What really excites him is the latest of the Fur Fabric ventures, into fleece. Using the flame resistant Courtelle, the fleece goes through all the usual knitting processes before being brushed with a wire brush to raise the surface, then given a foam backing. Until now the only real problem has been the lack of storage space, which has been solved by the completion of a new warehouse. Sharp went into the fleece market in 1984 and by the end of a year sales figures were up to 40,000 metres a week using producer dyed fibre and selling to customers like Marks & Spencer and Mothercare. Since everyone else piece dyes to order, the Dawson Fur Fabric method ensures greater continuity of quality and shade—one very good reason for the excellent results from the start.

There is no problem with the staff in any of the Fur Fabric factories since people never seem to want to leave. Jobs are never advertised. Managers are recruited from the shop floor and, in recent years, there has been a continuous intake from the local comprehensive school where Terry Sharp is in constant touch with the teachers. 'We have started a new tradition' he says 'and the school leavers have proved to be remarkably quick to learn.'

In an industry that can have its sticky times it is good to hear of a factory that is working to three-shift capacity. When Keith Fox joined Blackwood Brothers in 1978 he found that the mill required to be refurbished with machinery appropriate for the growing tufted industry with less emphasis on weaving.

Wilton was the earliest example of quality cut pile carpet and by the 1950s weaving started to give way to machine tufting. Gradually even the most traditional weavers in the carpet business were persuaded over to tufting, and clearly there was no future in trying to fight the change.

A vast investment policy was needed immediately and Dawson backed Fox all the way. Once the new factory, with the correct machines, was opened they soon adapted themselves to tufting and Blackwood went on at a pace, using much the same processes as for knitting yarn, taking raw wool, then blending, carding, spinning, twisting and reeling. The scale of everything is rather like Alice on the other side of the Looking Glass, with the huge three-kilo cones needed for carpet yarns and the hanks hanging to dry after dyeing looking immense compared to those used for knitting yarn.

Blackwood's figures leapt from 38 tonnes to 95 per week with 70 per cent of the yarn going to British carpet manufacturers. Next in the sales chart comes Scandinavia, with Denmark traditionally a strong market and most of the exported yarn coming back again as carpets. So far Belgium and Switzerland have been the most difficult and meticulous markets but Blackwoods are working on them.

The purchase of the Busby Spinning factory at Kilwinning near

Kilmarnock in October 1985 increased capacity by one third, taking production to 123 tonnes a week, and creating opportunities for expanding the range of yarns.

The Dawson managing directors are utterly sold on their own product and determined to transfer their enthusiasm to every visitor, but Allan Bouglas has to be the most convincing of them all. He is able to maintain a lengthy, informative, at times inspired, monologue on the merits of the unique British Replin jacquard tapestries, the pure wool cheviot tweed upholstery fabric, and most of all on the miracles of the machines invented by the founder of the company.

There are only 25 of these machines in the world and they are all down in the factory under the Bouglas office. It takes six months to train operatives and the only design limitation is in the head of the designer. There is no irregularity to the weave, the surface of which is the only one to be 100 per cent pure wool, and it is the only fabric in the world to have its own definition of the weave. British Replin supply the top end of the contract furnishing market, covering everything it is possible to imagine. Office equipment offers a large amount of volume with all manner of chairs and screens, followed by theatres, restaurants, hotels, the transport business from railway seats to upholstery for aircraft, hovercraft, jet foils, cruise liners, battleships, ferries, submarines. Anywhere the public congregate needs coverings of fabrics which meet strict smoke and flammability standards.

Going back to those cheviot tweeds, there are always some 40 colours in stock in pure new wool, ideal for offices all over the world. You will find British Replin cheviot in Marks & Spencer staff restaurants, in control rooms and crew quarters on oil rigs, in bingo halls and Barbican theatres. All require the same wearability and high standards of flammability tests. In one customer's building at 2 am one morning a fire in a catering kiosk melted various items, the polyester curtains 100 feet away disintegrated, but the seats only 10 feet away did not even ignite. Recently the question of flammability levels on fabrics has been of particular concern and British Replin have been working closely with all the airlines. For Boeing they have produced a unique wall covering with a low smoke level.

Special fabrics can be woven and crests or logos can be produced: indeed, they have been made for Lloyd's of London, for committee rooms in the Houses of Parliament, the Senate House at Strathclyde University, and for British Airways, where a metallic motif woven by British Replin was the only one to pass the aviation ignition tests.

Anyone, says Bouglas, can get the prestige jobs by charging next to nothing. His company is the only one to capture these markets on his own terms and to develop new markets. Today the company works in Japan, Germany, Italy, France, America and the

United Kingdom. Working with the airlines is like joining a circle of friends, with the members knowing one another all over the world. British Replin deals with all the major airlines but also with the smaller ones like Dan Air. There is a great deal of hard work involved, with many visits to find out exactly what each job needs and Bouglas spends much of his time sitting on his upholstery fabrics as he flies out to see customers. Those looms beneath his office have been working day and night resulting in an increase in turnover of 40 per cent in three years. Only natural fibres are used, with the emphasis on pure new wool, although there is a cashmere upholstery cloth at $700 a metre which Bouglas really enjoys making.

Luxury fibres are what Animal Fibres (Bradford) Limited are all about, since they deal in any fibre as long as it is the best, with the only exceptions cashmere and camelhair. The company was formed in 1977 to bring more speciality fibres into the group and to take advantage of the close ties with China, but it has extended beyond that initial brief. This is one of the youngest companies in Dawson International but already it is high on the list when it comes to profits per capita. You can count the members of the British-based team on two hands, though they make much use of the Swiss office in Zug. Managing director Tom Ross is in charge of sales and much of his time is spent travelling to visit suppliers and customers.

In charge of the Bradford office is Mrs Helen Cox who is responsible for administration and financial management and who is among the first of women directors appointed to any company within the group.

One of the major considerations for Animal Fibres is the stability, or more often the lack of it, in the currencies and politics of the supplying countries. Luxury yarns and fibres like alpaca, silk, mohair and angora have a habit of originating in the kind of countries where governments come and go, with an accompanying unease in financial markets. Coping with the ups and downs of currency is part of everyday life for Tom Ross. It is inevitable that prices become caught up in all this, taking one fibre up the scale one moment, another the next, but there is a cycle to be plotted by those who are as expert as this team combining British know-how and Swiss financial flair.

At least 70 per cent of Animal Fibre's business is exported and less than 10 per cent is involved with group members. Where there is close co-operation is with angora, which comes from China, is processed by Laidlaw & Fairgrieve, made up by Mackinnon and sold in Marks & Spencer.

The fibres handled by the company go mostly into the hand or machine knitting business, a large cake, as Tom Ross describes it, with enough to spare for Animal Fibres to expand.

A recent extension to their activity is the marketing of Cashgora. This is a new development, arising from the group

Kinross Cashmere Company, Adelong

Australian Certificate, Alan Smith

experimental farm in Australia, which involved the upgrading of the feral goat population by crossing the female feral with a male angora goat. The Australian feral goat is of mixed colour but the angora influence passes on the white genes. Work is now taking place to see if further on-breeding can result in future generations producing cashmere fibre. In the meantime this first cross fibre has been called Cashgora because it possesses some of the characteristics of both cashmere and mohair. Subsequent processing on the highly specialised machinery existing in the group has enabled Animal Fibres to produce a new luxury fibre for high fashion knitwear.

The research and development department started in 1961, with its major briefs the solving of problems and the maintenance of quality, particularly on any new process installed. Objective measurements were decided upon for fibres, yarns and garments. Software is prepared within the department for various programmes to help with production monitoring and control throughout the group. Energy efficiency is mandatory with any manufacturing process and is monitored frequently. A totally new concept in dyeing and drying animal fibres has been launched under the Fastran mark, aiding the continuous search for improvement in manufacturing methods with energy savings.

These are exciting developments and will add to the profitability of this already remarkable company. They owe much to the energy and enthusiasm of Geoffrey Smith, who holds some unique titles. He is the Number One Life Member of the Cashmere Producers of New Zealand, and the second to become a member of the Australian Cashmere Goat Association, the first being, of course, Sir Alan Smith.

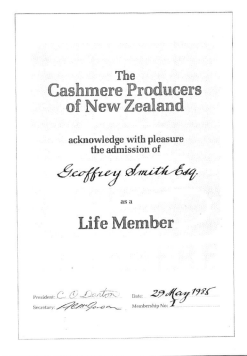

New Zealand Certificate, Geoff Smith

Dawson Overseas

The overseas division of the group has long played an active part in Dawson affairs. The Swiss sales office under the direction of Herman Stutz assists all group members with exports into the European area and advises on currency handling.

Fred Moylan in Australia has his hands full with the cashmere goat and sheep breeding programme, generally holding a watching brief on raw material supplies.

The Hong Kong office has been busy in quite different directions. That teeming, exhilarating place is now the home of Roger Rankin, who not only worked in the Pringle sales office in Sackville Street, London, in the late 1960s but married the Pringle designer at that time, the then Lesley Brown. They spent some time in New York for Dawson and were the ideal people to have around when the group decided to set up a manufacturing unit in Kowloon to make shetland sweaters at the right price to suit the American market. The yarn came from Laidlaw & Fairgrieve and design expertise emanated from Pringle and Braemar. Since the Rankins went to Hong Kong in 1977, the Kowloon operation has expanded to supply the Caribbean, Bermuda and Japan.

Hong Kong Sales Office

Charles Scott went out to South Africa for a year to run a manufacturing unit which would make Pringle sweaters under licence. He, like Roger Rankin, was a Pringle man. He had gone into the office one morning and, before he had time for a cup of coffee, was asked if he would like to move to South Africa right away. He rang his wife to discuss it with her, she said she would back him whatever he decided and by lunchtime everything was arranged for the year's stay in South Africa. That was in 1969 and Charlie Scott, with his family of three sons and two daughters, is still there, based in Johannesburg.

The New York office in Broadway has a compact unit led by Ray Donnelly. It opened in 1975 as a marketing and distribution base for the Braemar International ranges coming from Hong Kong and has since been extended to take in production from other parts of the world. The design, production and sales team work together to create a collection that retains the Scottish tradition but adds the necessary touch of American styling. The main difference between the American and the European ranges lies in the use of colour and detail, but having a resident designer trained in Scotland who understands his market without losing sight of his origins has given Dawson a major asset.

Ronald Miller made his intentions clear regarding the future direction of Dawson International when he acquired Kammgarnspinnerei Wilhelmshaven AG, one of Germany's largest producers of hand-knitting wools. It was Miller's first acquisition and it was the first really big buy for the group since 1979.

In the north of Germany, on the shores of the North Sea, Kammgarnspinnerei Wilhelmshaven AG was founded on 22nd July 1949 as Kammgarnspinnerie und Weberei Wilhelmshaven Aktiengesellschaft with a capital of DM 1 million.

View of KSW, Wilhelmshaven, West Germany

Production of hand and machine knitting yarn started in 1950 in the scantily restored rooms of a former shipyard, followed a year later by a small weaving mill. A lack of sufficient finance and periods of indifferent sales led to several years of problems, heightened by the fact that a shortage of capital meant that the company was having to manage with out of date machinery. Eventually this made the weaving side of the business so uncompetitive that it was closed.

During the year 1st April 1965 to 31st March 1966 the 600 employees produced a turnover of DM 23.4 million, the majority of the business being in hand-knitting yarn. Cash contributions increased the stock capital to DM 4 million.

In 1965 Wolfgang Inderhees was appointed to the executive board, one year later becoming chairman. It was the arrival of Inderhees that rejuvenated the company, and results showed consistent improvement. In 1966 the company's name was changed to Kammgarnspinnerei Wilhelmshaven Aktiengesellschaft. In 1968 production started on Tuffi bathroom carpets.

From 1974 strong steps were taken to establish the newly introduced hand knitting Hübner Wolle brand to the market. After a first success a setback occurred in distribution, caused by the dependence on wholesalers. Inderhees set up an independent marketing organisation in 1983 to supply the retail trade direct.

The '70s and '80s were a period of strong growth, high capital expenditure and profits which were well above those gained by their competitors. Since the company was formed investments have amounted to DM 72 million and at present the whole plant is valued at approximately DM 60 million.

More than half the hand-knitting yarn sold in Germany is imported from over 30 different countries. KSW's share of the total hand-knitting yarn consumption is some 13 per cent and its share of the inland production of worsted hand knitting comes to more than 25 per cent.

Inderhees has remained at the head of KSW since the Dawson takeover and his knowledge of the German market has been invaluable in the discussions that have taken place on the expansion of Hübner Wolle, to be concentrated at first within its home market.

KSW, with its extensive dyeing and spinning operation and workforce of over a thousand, is producing 4 million kilos of worsted yarn, of which Hübner accounts for a small percentage at present; but Dawson plans are to redress the balance in the near future, leaning more heavily towards the branded quality yarn which is marketed under the slogan, *Stride Mit Chic,* or *Knit in Style.* There is no doubt that other brand names will be launched in due course. The small production of tufted bath mats will also be retained.

The Dawson management feel strongly about the benefit of having your own man on the spot and the wisdom of this was proved with Miller's next acquisition.

Philip Kemp was the man Miller turned to in 1983 when he decided to step into the American market. British-born Kemp had worked in the States for many years and is a marketing man with experience gained by working with Boots, Cussons and the Guinness group. Kemp scoured the United States looking for the right company. It had to fulfil the usual criteria set by Dawson: it must be in textiles, it must be stable, the management must be right. He studied dozens until he came up with the JE Morgan Knitting Mills, begun in 1945 by Morgan and his wife Anna.

John E Morgan, a native of Tamaqua, Pennsylvania, came into the textile industry at 13 years old, working in the cutting department of a local underwear plant. While there he learned the fundamentals of taking care of machinery. His next position was as a machinist with the Reidler Knitting Mills, an underwear plant in Hazleton, Pennsylvania. His wife, Mrs Anna Morgan, also worked for the Reidler Company.

Morgan Knitting Mills, Pennsylvania, USA

In 1945 John and his wife opened their first underwear company as a partnership in a building behind a bakery on Row Street in Tamaqua, later moving to larger headquarters at the Acme Store building. At the same time, John Morgan purchased the Center Street building (the present site of the company's outlet store and, incidentally, the location of the plant in which he worked as a youth). There he set up his knitting operation with a staff of 65. As the business expanded Morgan moved his entire operation to the building on Center Street.

The Morgan Company became a corporation known as the JE Morgan Knitting Mills Inc in 1954, with officers John E Morgan, president; Anna Morgan, vice president and treasurer; and Elmira Fegley, secretary. In the same year the first sales office was set up in the Empire State Building.

Morgan was awarded patent rights on his invention of circular thermal fabric in 1958. This invention revitalized the winter weight underwear business in the United States. At the same time Morgan purchased the building at East Broad Street, used exclusively for the manufacturing of the new thermal products.

A dream was realized in 1969 when the company moved to the new plant in Hometown, the present home of the Morgan company. This is a completely integrated operation from knitting yarn to the shipment of the finished product. There are additional plants at Tower City, Williamstown, Gilbertsville and Valley View, Pennsylvania, necessitated by the increasing demand for Morgan products.

Sadly, Anna Morgan died but John Morgan and Elmira Fegley remain, very much involved with the company. John Morgan is a natural born engineer whose ideas and genius led his company to the peak, for Morgans are now the biggest producers of thermal underwear in America.

Customers are all the major chains—among them J C Penney, Sears and K-mart—with merchandise shipped 2,600 miles west to Los Angeles, 2,000 miles south to El Paso, Texas and 1,400 miles north to Milwaukee. Most goods move by road, 3,000 dozen to the truckful.

John Morgan is a strong man, a force to be reckoned with and never lost for words. His sayings are as famous as those of Alan Smith in Scotland. Some of his most quoted include 'If I want to know what's going on, I just talk to the janitor for five minutes', and 'Long winded meetings are a waste of time. Keep it short and get back to work'. But perhaps the favourite is 'One thing you can always say about me, I'm humble.'

Ronald Miller visited the factories on Philip Kemp's recommendation and made his decision to buy Morgans for US $41.5 million, the largest amount ever invested in a takeover by the group. There were observers who could not see the benefits in the acquisition, but Miller has far-sighted plans which will include

Knitting at Morgan Knitting Mills

greater involvement in the biggest growth area, leisurewear. He installed his own man Philip Kemp as president and chief executive with John Morgan as chairman. Kemp's worth was demonstrated immediately when he repackaged the Morgan baby blanket, a product that inexplicably was not selling as it should. The new packaging took it straight into top sales. John Embrey is convinced that having Kemp in the market, concentrating 100 per cent on finding the right company in which to invest was the reason why the purchase has been such a success.

In September of 1984, the year that Dawson purchased JE Morgan, the Prime Minister, Margaret Thatcher, and her husband visited Todd & Duncan. The following year Ronald Miller received the CBE for his services to Scottish industry and also, it is to be hoped, in appreciation of his boldness in developing his own section of it.

The Future of
Dawson International

No changes are indicated in the way the group has steered its many areas of activity towards a coherent position in the specialist business market. Ronald Miller intends to follow the established pattern. Every year each managing director, accompanied by his management team, meets with the Kinross team to discuss the plans for the coming year and prepare a framework within which that particular company will work. Budgets are agreed and production forecasts evaluated. Profits are expected to be made, but managing directors are left to achieve them. After their meeting each managing director should feel he can now get on with his job, although should he need a quick decision he can get one at any time.

John Embrey is more than happy with this and the fact that, though the group is considerably larger than it was when he was in the accounts department, the team is smaller, so there is no delay in decision making. He is adamant that centralisation causes a blockage and that cannot be good for any business. Nevertheless, he admits that he does like to be kept in the picture by each company, if only to reassure himself. The need for a quick decision is one matter that need never worry a managing director. If he feels he needs to invest in some new machinery, or anything from an additional designer to an extension to the factory, he will get a sympathetic hearing and, usually, the go-ahead to spend the money.

Like Miller, Embrey is an imaginative financial man. Investment is the key to success in his opinion, and it must be a continuous process. Neglect in replacing outdated machinery for even a year can result in a horrendous cost the following year, by which time another piece of equipment may need replacing. Embrey's attitude is that it is far better to buy a new machine every year so that it can earn its keep. He is convinced that it is essential to take a much more flexible attitude to finance. 'There is' he says, 'still too much negative thinking about spending money in British business.'

Ask the managing directors in Dawson International what John Waterton's job is and they will quite likely say that they don't know how exactly to define it but he is very good at it. They will

Neidpath Castle, Peebles, built in the 14th century
Scottish Tourist Board

also comment on his fluency in several European languages.

What is clear is that Waterton's travels take him around the world meeting customers and agents, an exercise from which he can pick up any local problems. Watching out for potential trouble in any of the Dawson companies is also his role. He takes the view that anyone reasonably competent can manage when all is well; but good management means coping if you have a crisis on your hands, when you must get up and do something about it. He asserts that it is up to the managing directors to face up to any troubles and to judge if the business is slipping off the track which they set for themselves and which the Dawson board approved. He admits that it is sometimes easier to see these things happening, and at a very early stage, when you are outside and away from day to day events.

The essential course of action both for the managing directors and for the Dawson management team when things are definitely not working must be to 'face up to it, cut it, and don't be sentimental. When my colleagues mutter about my attitude I tell them that this is what is called management by provocation', Waterton will explain, unabashed.

Ronald Miller quotes the Scottish whisky trade as his guide to marketing. It is the high quality, high priced single malts that never cease to sell, whatever the competition may be. He sees Dawson International as moving in specialist areas within which it is important to make changes at the right moment, as the customers change.

Miller is maintaining the traditions established by Sir Alan Smith of going out himself to visit both suppliers and customers, joining David Blackburn every other year on his visits to China, and thereby taking advantage of the high regard in which Blackburn is clearly held.

When he makes these trips Miller will be promoting not just the Dawson International approach to business life but his home country. He has great feeling for Scotland and regrets that not enough is conveyed beyond the Borders about the knowledge and skill that has accumulated in Scottish industry, ready for anyone with the imagination to invest in the best in design. He is realistic enough to know that the most difficult task is to encourage the Scots to think in the longer term and is especially aware of the need for them to persist in making themselves better known to the world outside.

'The Scottish businessmen today are always travelling, so while they are at it they should be promoting their country everywhere they go. It is unique, after all, there is only one Scotland—and with a reputation for standards of quality rather than volume. Not enough is made of that.' Clearly, those engaged in trying to break through the Scots' natural aversion to promotion have found another ally in Ronald Miller. He sees knitwear as one of Scotland's modern craft industries and feels that Dawson

The Scottish Borders
Scottish Tourist Board

International has an important role to play in maintaining the standards.

The management team should be assured that their methods work. In 1983 productivity in terms of added value was over £10,000 per employee, a figure which Miller was proud to announce to shareholders as significantly higher than the average over the whole of the United Kingdom textile industry.

Neither Smith nor Miller will have anything to do with talk of increased international competition. Opportunities are there, and the Dawson International aim is to set out to grab them, with nothing spared in terms of investment.

The home base is not ignored. Quite apart from the huge amounts invested each year, note is taken of the employment situation. Despite all the new machinery, with its hi-tech, labour saving assets installed in the British factories, employment has risen, with over 1,000 new jobs being created in Scotland alone during the last three years.

The training of future managers is helped by the establishment of two degree course scholarships with the Scottish College of Textiles at Galashiels. Joint sponsorship degree course programmes are arranged in combination with Marks & Spencer among others; while, in America, Dawson International takes part in the Walt Disney World Showroom Fellowship in Florida.

Ronald Miller feels it is important that the group grows organically, from within, with the addition of some careful acquisitions. Much has been learned from the mistakes of the past and any future buys will be in the textile area, however broad that base may be, because that is where their strengths lie. Future buys will only be where there is a well-managed company with a good track record. An essential extra is that the people and the chemistry must be right. John Embrey is adamant that it was the mutual respect and sympathy between Morgan himself and Ronald Miller that clinched that particular deal.

Germany, America and the United Kingdom are seen as the kernel, the three areas in which there can be development in the immediate future. In America, for example, there is abundant spending power and there could, perhaps should, be a deeper involvement. Japan is another strong, growing industrial area which cannot be ignored, with many of the Dawson companies exporting there to a great degree. But what to buy is a decision that cannot be made overnight. Miller and his team are only too aware that every step they take today will affect what happens tomorrow.

It is always possible in a constantly changing world that business could drop down into the doldrums again, as it did in the 1970s, but it is even more likely that the structure of the company today will keep it buoyant through low spells. Some future development in the management is bound to happen as the group continues its expansion.

The whole concept of Dawson International has been an outward looking view from Scotland. The success of the group's trading efforts has been recognised by the Queen's Award for Export Achievement in 1983, following a previous award in 1979. In addition, many other companies in the group have also received such awards in past years. The work in developing overseas markets has been immense. It takes a long time to establish contacts and confidence amongst overseas companies before success pays off. In the last few years, international trading has become even more intense, and to be successful on a continuing basis it is no longer possible to limit manufacturing to one particular area of the world. It was through recognising this that acquisitions were made in Germany and the United States in 1983 and 1984. These acquisitions are specialist companies in their own fields and give the group a broader manufacturing base, but they also open up the product range substantially. KSW and Morgan already account for some 20 per cent of total group profits. Whatever happens, any future purchase will be for positive reasons, not simply to remove rivals. Dawson International are not in the business of buying up competitors.

The last word should go to the man who made the moves that led to Dawson International, Sir Alan Smith. Talking about the future several years ago, he reiterated his belief in quality. Summing up the need for British textile companies to remain vigilant about maintaining standards he said 'Desire for fine products is not confined to Western Nations—all of Eastern Europe and Asia will eventually offer us selling opportunities'.

Dawson International will be there when the time is right.